General "Mad" Anthony Wayne & The Battle of Fallen Timbers

A Look at Some Key Events
in the Life and Times of General Wayne

Arthur R. Bauman

authorHOUSE®

AuthorHouse™
1663 Liberty Drive
Bloomington, IN 47403
www.authorhouse.com
Phone: 1-800-839-8640

First published by AuthorHouse   12/9/2010

ISBN: 978-1-4520-9371-0 (sc)
ISBN: 978-1-4520-9372-7 (e)

Library of Congress Control Number: 2010916441

Printed in the United States of America

This book is printed on acid-free paper.

Certain stock imagery © Thinkstock.

This book is dedicated to . . .

The brave and hearty settlers in Ohio Country, especially those who lived there during the Northwest Indian War from 1785 to 1795. Also known as Little Turtle's War, it pitted the Western Confederacy against the United States for control of the Northwest Territory.
The United States military forces that fought the various battles for the territory from 1790 to 1794.
The Indians who, as an indirect result of the Treaty of Greenville, were forced into Kansas as settlers continued their westward push.

~~A. Bauman

Contents

Photographs/Drawings

From the author . . .

While attending Kent State University in Ashtabula, Ohio, in 1975, I took a course on Ohio history taught by Dr. Richard C. Knopf, author of *Anthony Wayne: a Name in Arms.* Knopf was an expert on the Connecticut Western Reserve (in what is now a small corner of northeastern Ohio) and on the major Indian battles in Ohio.

When talking about the Battle of Fallen Timbers on Aug. 20, 1794, Knopf said, General "Mad" Anthony Wayne's personality was comparable to that of General "Stormin" Norman Schwarzkopf. Others have described him the same way. I believe Wayne's personality was similar to that of World War II hero, General George Patton. All were shrewd and showed no fear of the enemy.

Wayne was a national figure in a forgotten conflict. The Northwest Indian War (1785-1795) was over land in the Northwest Territory, which Britain ceded to the United States at the end of the Revolutionary War. The final battle was August 20, 1794, when General "Mad" Anthony Wayne defeated Little Turtle at the Battle of Fallen Timbers. Wayne died in 1796 at the age of 51.

Date, name, and place information varies by source. I have used information that could be verified by at least two sources. Wayne's name appears three ways: "Mad Anthony Wayne," "Mad Anthony" Wayne, and "Mad" Anthony Wayne. I have chosen to use the last form because his given name was Anthony Wayne.

~~A. Bauman

<u>Prologue</u>

T he area east of the Mississippi River and south of the Great Lakes was a continuing battleground for Indians and settlers beginning in the 1600s and continuing into the early 1800s. The French sided with the Algonquin-speaking tribes in battles with members of the Iroquois Confederation and their Dutch allies in the New Netherland colony in what has become known as the Beaver Wars from 1650 to about 1700. Some call those wars the bloodiest in North American history.

Eventually, aided by their Dutch allies that provided blankets, knives, hatchets, and other firearms, the Iroquois almost eliminated the Huron Indians and all the Indians west of their lands in the Northwest Territory or Ohio Country. Most of the Iroquois didn't live in Ohio Territory; they ventured into the area to hunt beaver or deer before returning to their homes in the East.

The battles between Indians and various European peoples or between Europeans and colonists continued on and off from the time the first settlers set foot on the continent. As the settlers looked to head west, Ohio Country became one of the prime areas of conflict, leading to battles, treaties, broken promises, and more warfare. The Battle of Fallen Timbers and the Treaty of Greenville, in 1794 and 1795 respectively, ended ten years of almost constant conflict — not necessarily organized military confrontations — between the American settlers and the Indians over the Ohio Country. General "Mad" Anthony Wayne led the victorious American troops in the battle and signed the treaty on behalf of the United States.

Little Turtle, chief of the Miami Indians, signed on behalf of the Indians. Following the treaty he tried to keep his tribe at peace while protecting the tribe's land from white settlers eager to move west.

***

Wayne was born January 1, 1745, in Easttown Township, Chester County near present-day Paoli, Pennsylvania. Because of his mathematical aptitude, he was educated as a surveyor in his uncle's private academy in Philadelphia. In 1765 Benjamin Franklin and others sent him to Nova Scotia to survey their land and document all of the natural resources.

Wayne returned the following year, developed the farm near Waynesboro, Pennsylvania, worked in his father's tannery operation, and continued his surveying work. He was married in 1767. He soon became a leader in Chester County and was elected to serve in the Pennsylvania Legislature from 1774 to 1775.

***

Little Chief, hailed as the last chief of the Miami Indians, was born circa 1752 (some historians say 1747) near what is present-day Fort Wayne, Indiana. He was a chief of Atchatchakangouen division of the Miami tribe; his Indian name was Michikinikwa. He helped the British in the American Revolutionary but little else is known about him prior to 1790.

He later became famous for his military prowess and formidable attacks on the white settlers in Ohio Country and the United States Army following the creation of the Northwest Territory in 1787.

Following the defeat of the Indians in the Battle of Fallen Timbers he refused to take part in battles against the Americans. He became a friend of the Americans and met George Washington in 1797. Some historians say Washington gave him a ceremonial sword, which he cherished until his death July 14, 1812, in Fort Wayne.

Chapter One
Extension of American Revolution

Wayne Joins War in 1775

Anthony Wayne raised a militia at the outset of the American Revolution and in 1776 became colonel of the 4th Pennsylvania Regiment. His regiment was part of the Continental Army's unsuccessful attempt to invade Canada, where he was sent to assist Benedict Arnold. Wayne led a rear-guard action at the Battle of Trois–Rivieres (Three Rivers) on June 6, 1776. The last major battle on Quebec soil, it was part of the American colonists' invasion of Quebec that started in 1775 to liberate Quebec from the British.

The Quebec militia spotted the American troops crossing the Saint Lawrence and alerted British troops at Trois-Rivieres. A local farmer led the Americans into a swamp, giving the British a chance to get additional forces into the village and set up positions behind the Americans.

Some of the Americans, led by General William Thompson, made their way out of the swamp only to be driven back. After a brief exchange of fire the men broke and ran leaving guns and supplies behind.

Wayne formed a rear guard of about 800 men to attack the British but they were also driven back into the woods. Some avenues of retreat were cut off with the British taking a large number of prisoners. Wayne was wounded in the leg, resulting in a slight limp.

Following the defeat, the remainder of the American forces, under the command of General John Sullivan, retreated first to Fort Saint-Jean and then to Fort Ticonderoga. About 1700 Continental Army troops under Wayne's command spent part of the winter of 1776-77 at Fort Ticonderoga.

British Foil Americans Again

On February 21, 1777, Wayne was commissioned by General George Washington and rose to the rank of brigadier general. He joined Washington in New Jersey on September 11, 1777.

Wayne commanded a force at Chadd's Ford on the Brandywine River on the Pennsylvania-Delaware border where he fought British and Hessian troops under the command of Baron von Knyphausen until nightfall.

Because Washington had received faulty information, the Americans were forced to pull back from the Brandywine fords under attack by forces led by Sir William Howe, commander-in-chief of the British forces in America, and General Charles Cornwallis, a British general and later a colonial governor.

Wayne unsuccessfully contested the advance of Knyphausen's Hessian and British troops that crossed the Brandywine at Chadd's Ford. After fighting three hours to turn back the British, Wayne withdrew to the rear of General Nathanael Greene's troops

Following the American retreats at the Battle of Brandywine and the Battle of the Clouds in the Campaign for Philadelphia, Washington left a force under the command of Wayne behind to monitor and harass the British as they prepared to move on the revolutionary capital. Under the false assumption the British were unaware of his presence Wayne stationed his troops close to the enemy.

On the evening of September 20-21, British forces under the command of Major General Charles Grey led a surprise attack on Wayne's encampment in the area the Paoli Tavern, near present-day Malvern.

Grey ensured the surprise by having his troops remove the flints from their muskets, earning him the nickname, "No Flint" Grey. He ordered his troops not to fire but to use their weapons as clubs. The 7th Pennsylvania Regiment was at the end of the column, which was at the head of the attack. The Americans sustained three hundred casualties in what became known as the Paoli Massacre.

Wayne part of attack on Germantown

Defeats at Brandywine and Paoli left Philadelphia defenseless; Cornwallis seized it on September 16, 1777. Howe left roughly 3500 men to defend the city and moved nearly 10,000 to Germantown. With the British forces split, Washington was trying to maneuver his troops into a favorable position to launch an attack against the British to take Germantown. His plan was to strike with four columns, one under the command of Wayne.

On October 3, they began their nighttime assault but the darkness made communicating difficult. At first the American troops were not detected by the outer guards; it appeared the Americans would be victorious however slow troop movement left them without the element of surprise.

Hindered by a thick fog that hung over the battlefield all day as well as smoke from cannons and muskets, Greene's column became confused. One of the brigades wandered off course and collided with Wayne's brigade and mistook them for redcoats. The two brigades opened fire on each other, became more disoriented, and fled.

The main attack failed and the British routed the fleeing Americans for nine miles before giving into the resistance to Greene's infantry and Wayne's artillery guns and a detachment of dragoons.

In early October 1777 the Americans were on the verge of victory in the Battle of Germantown when the tide turned and they retreated west to White Marsh, Gulph Mills, eventually reaching Valley Forge on December 19.

Wayne's Troops Winter at Valley Forge

The defeat at Georgetown was especially disheartening. The Americans were starving. The conditions were bitterly cold. Some of the troops had shoes that were worn through. They had no pay and very little to eat.

Washington made the decision to spend the winter in Valley Forge on the Schuylkill River, about twenty-two miles from Philadelphia. He had 1000 huts constructed for at least 12,000 troops, including Wayne's men. The cramped quarters were damp and cold.

The troops spent the winter in a miserable, never-ending hell. The weather was so cold the river froze. There were no blankets, shoes or warm clothes. Food supplies were low. The men survived on a diet of fire cakes made of flour and water. Typhus, dysentery, typhoid fever, and pneumonia killed 2000 people. The animals starved or froze to death.

Washington, who remained with his troops, feared that an army in such dire conditions might not be able to survive, let alone fight.

In February 1778, Washington sent Wayne to New Jersey in search of food. He and his troops had minor skirmishes with the British before returning to camp with food and shoes. Wayne's numerous appeals to the Pennsylvania authorities for help went unanswered until April.

Prussian Whips Troops into Shape

On February 23, 1778, Baron Friedrich Wilhelm von Steuben, a former Prussian staff officer who had volunteered to assist the Americans, arrived at Valley Forge. Because he had a reputation as an outstanding training officer Washington gave him the job of drilling the troops. Many had little training because of the lack of time and too many skirmishes and were ill-prepared to face the British.

With the help of Greene and Colonel Alexander Hamilton, von Steuben established a training regimen that turned the Continental Army into a well-trained and capable fighting force by the time it left Valley Forge.

On June 18, 1778, Washington and his troops left their winter quarters, and six days later Wayne's troops were within a few miles of the British troops who had pulled out of Philadelphia. At a war council Wayne convinced a reluctant Washington to attack immediately.

He led the American attack at the Battle of Monmouth. Wayne and his troops were outnumbered and pinned down by the British forces. However, he held out until Washington sent reinforcements; a scene that would later play out again in the Southern Campaign.

The British under the leadership of Cornwallis had seized the initiative because of Major General Charles Lee's unsteady handling of lead Continental elements. Washington had ordered Lee to attack the retreating troops during the Battle of Monmouth but Lee ordered a retreat into Washington's advancing troops.

Washington's timely arrival on the battlefield on June 28 rallied the main part of the Continental Army, including Wayne's troops, in an attack on the rear column of the British Army. Washington fought his opponent to a draw after a pitched battle but Cornwallis succeeded in protecting the main part of the British army from further attack.

Monmouth marked the first major success for Washington. The battle improved the military reputations of Washington, Marquis de Lafayette, who had greatly improved discipline and morale among the troops, and Wayne.

It ended Lee's career; he would later force court-martial.

British Fortify Stony Point

The British had built Stony Point, a strong fort at King's Ferry, on the west side of the Hudson River as an important part of its defense.

It sat on a rocky bluff 150 feet above the water, which surrounded it on three sides; the fourth connected the point to the mainland by a narrow marsh that was submerged at high tide. The British had constructed a series of redoubts and strategically placed several cannons to protect the fort.

Lieutenant Colonel Henry Johnston was in charge of 500 to 700 well-armed, well-trained men garrisoned at the fort. (The number varies by source.) The fortification was manned by British troops and a gunboat positioned to protect the river approaches. A sloop also patrolled that part of the river.

Washington watched the construction through a telescope from a nearby mountain. Some historians believe he also gathered information on the garrison's strength, watchwords, and sentries from local merchants.

The fort was protected only by earthen walls for cannon placements and trees sharpened to a point (abatis) and placed 50 yards out to protect from water attack along the narrow beach at the end of the point.

Although that abatis appeared to be a good idea, planners failed to take into account that at low tide the trees were easily visible and troops could simply walk around the ends.

Wayne Alters Attack Plan

Washington planned a nighttime two-pronged pincer attack with 1200 men, generally not enough to overtake a well-prepared defensive position. However the low tide gave Washington and his troops the edge. Washington gave Wayne his orders with permission to alter them as he found necessary, something he rarely did.

Washington knew Wayne had a natural ability to control others, a non-tiring determination to keep on fighting and a strict sense of value that kept him always forging ahead. Some historians believe Washington gave Wayne permission to change orders because of his tactical abilities. The men had to scale the steep, rocky sides of Stony Point and attack with only bayonets to prevent a musket blast to alert the British.

Wayne devised a plan to overtake the cannons and the fort. He made only one adjustment to the plan: he added a third prong using a small force to approach the fortification on the marsh side, which was exactly what the British anticipated.

Wayne told the column led by Major Harvey Murfree to approach with loaded muskets and maintain firing at a pace "sufficient to amuse the enemy." Colonel Richard Butler led the northern column and Wayne led the southern column.

Wayne Attacks at Night

Washington instructed Wayne to make the night assault on the fort with the Light Infantry Brigade made up of about 1300 carefully selected soldiers from Connecticut, Massachusetts, Pennsylvania, Virginia, and North Carolina. Wayne didn't tell his soldiers, but he regarded the attack as a suicide mission. He left instructions for the care of his family and his reputation should he die in the battle.

The three columns left West Point at nightfall July 15, 1779. Civilians encountered en route were taken into custody to keep them from alerting the British of the pending attack. The columns gathered about 10 p.m. at a farm just south of the fortification. Each man pinned a piece of white paper to his hat to identify him from the British in the dark.

Weather was in favor of the Continentals as they moved out; heavy clouds cut off the moonlight and high winds forced the ships to leave their posts at Stony Point and move down river in order to keep from being smashed against the rocks.

The assault began at midnight July 15-16, when the Americans mounted an attack using primarily fixed bayonets with the exception of Major Hardy Murfree's battalion that attacked the center of the fortification as a diversionary tactic. Wayne's men had no loaded weapons or artillery support in order to preserve the element of surprise.

Wayne Takes Fort in about an Hour

The attack began at midnight, and as planned Murfree's unit was spotted by the sentries and commenced firing on the British troops. The light from the muzzle of a cannon blast at Murfree's unit revealed Wayne's column but by that time it was too late for the British to turn the cannon. Wayne's troops were inside the fortification. A spent musket ball hit Wayne in the head, taking him out of action and leaving the column under the command of Colonel Christian Febiger. Butler's column had cut their way through the abatis, suffering the only loss of American lives.

About an hour after the attack began, the Americans claimed victory as they met inside the fort and witnessed the British surrender in one of the greatest American victories of the Revolutionary War. Between 480 and 550 British were captured — 75 of the injured — and between 20 and 63 killed. (Numbers vary by source.)

Only 15 Americans were killed; Wayne was not among them — he suffered only a minor scalp wound. Another 83 were injured. On their way out the American troops seized needed supplies and destroyed the fort. It proved to be the major engagement of 1779 and one of the last battles in the Northern Theatre.

Before dawn Wayne sent a brief dispatch to Washington telling him of the victory. Washington rode in the next day to review the battlefield and congratulate the troops. For his part, Wayne received a Gold Medal from Congress, one of the few awarded during the Revolutionary War.

Wayne's victory at Stony Point, New York, on July 15, 1779, was the highlight of his Revolutionary War service. British forces had begun building fortifications on the west side of the Hudson River in June in an effort to draw Washington's troops out of West Point.

British Take Defensive Position

As a result of the American success at Stony Point and the threat it created, the British were pushed into a defensive position around New York City and also turned their attention to an offensive campaign in the south that would end in defeat at Yorktown.

In January 1781 the Pennsylvania Line mutinied, but Wayne interceded and restored the composure of the Army. It was during that year that he acquired the nickname "Mad" because of his fiery temperament. He demanded obedience and loyalty. His temper flared if anyone hinted at incompetence or questioned his honor.

The story goes that when a man Wayne occasionally used as a spy wound up in jail for disorderly conduct the man demanded he be freed because he was a friend of Wayne's. When the local constables refused, the man insisted Wayne would demand his release. When word reached Wayne, his legendary temper flared and he refused.

Hearing of his refusal the part-time spy muttered, "Anthony Wayne is mad … Mad Anthony that's what he is." It is said that the tale made its way through the Continental Army and the name stuck.

The following month Washington ordered Wayne to head south but Wayne was detained in York, Pennsylvania, until May. He met Lafayette's forces on June 7 at Fredericksburg, Virginia, and the combined troops were to attack and ensure the surrender of Cornwallis.

Wayne was later victorious at West Point, New York, but on July 6, 1781, he was ambushed at Green Springs by the British Army during the last major battle of the Virginia Campaign before Yorktown.

British Ambush Wayne's Troops

Lafayette was following the retreating troops under the leadership of Cornwallis as they moved from Williamsburg to Yorktown. He planned to attack a small British rear guard after the majority of the troops had been ferried south at Jamestown.

At 3 in the afternoon Lafayette sent out an advance guard of 800 troops under Wayne's leadership, not knowing that Cornwallis had concealed the bulk of his troops in the woods. Wayne had no idea his 800 men were facing the entire British army of 5000 men.

The American riflemen pushed forward until they were forced to retreat by the sheer numbers of the British. The American militia on the left retreated; the Pennsylvania Line on the left retreated; the Pennsylvania Line on the right stubbornly retired.

Wayne realized he was in a dangerous trap and would be overwhelmed before the rest of the American Army could arrive. He organized a bayonet charge. The British temporarily recoiled allowing Wayne to disengage and retreat. Hearing the sound of the battle, Lafayette had drawn some of his troops up a half mile behind Wayne. The British did not pursue the retreating Americans but continued loading their troops on transports to Portsmouth and later Yorktown.

The American forces eventually succeeded in blocking Cornwallis and his men by land and sea. On October 19, 1781, Cornwallis surrendered to Washington and Lafayette at Yorktown.

Sir Henry Clinton from Britain remained in New York, astonished, embarrassed, and unable to accept defeat of the world's greatest Army. The British defeat was also an embarrassment to King George III.

Although the American victory at Yorktown is often called the final battle of the American Revolution, the southern colonies remained under attack by the British for several months. The American Revolution continued under the command of Greene who trapped the British, then returned to ambush them.

Wayne Forces British to Surrender

After the surrender of Cornwallis, Wayne was sent to Georgia and South Carolina to secure the surrender of the British troops. His first objective was to take control of Savannah, Georgia. Following several battles, the British evacuated the city on July 11, 1782.

Wayne's next stop was in South Carolina. After the British left Charleston, Wayne marched into the city. By April 1783, the Treaty of Paris was signed; the United States was recognized as a nation.

Wayne stayed with the Army until his retirement in October 1783 when he returned home to Waynesboro, Pennsylvania, worn out from the rigors of war and in poor health.

He was promoted to major general on October 10, 1783, and following the war returned to Pennsylvania where he served in the State Legislature in 1784. After his year in the Legislature, he moved to Georgia and settled on land given to him by the state as a thank-you for his military efforts. He eventually lost the plantation because of money problems. While in Georgia, he was a delegate to the state convention that ratified the Constitution in 1788.

In 1791 he was a U.S. Representative in the Second United States Congress but lost his seat in a debate about his residency qualifications; he declined to seek re-election.

In 1792 Washington appointed him Commander-in-Chief of the United States Army to subdue the Indians in the Northwest Territory.

Chapter Two
Before Fallen Timbers

Series of conflicts begins in 1640s

The Battle of Fallen Timbers on Aug. 20, 1794, and the resulting Treaty of Greenville, signed August 2, 1795, marked the end of the Northwest Indian War — also known as Little Turtle's War and other names — that began in 1785.

The internal war was between the United States and a confederation comprised of a number of American Indian tribes for control of the Northwest Territory, an area covering 260,000 square miles west of Pennsylvania and northwest of the Ohio River. It covered all of the modern states of Ohio, Indiana, Illinois, Michigan, and Wisconsin, as well as the northeastern part of Minnesota.

The war followed centuries of conflict over this territory, first among Indian nations, and then with the added shifting alliances among the tribes and European powers, France and Great Britain and their colonists.

As a result of the Beaver Wars, the Iroquois expanded their territory and destroyed several tribal confederacies, pushing the tribes across the Mississippi River. Nearly all the native tribes of the Ohio Country (sometimes called the Ohio Territory) were forced to flee or were killed, leaving behind empty villages and decimated tribes.

In 1655 the Iroquois became trading partners with the British. By the early 1700s, tribes began returning to the Northwest Territory but without their former strong alliances.

United States Looks West

During the eighteenth century the United States, facing difficult times, was looking toward westward expansion into what was then Northwestern Ohio creating tension with the Indians who had been threatened by the arrival of European colonists hundreds of years earlier.

The Indians relied on fire; the Europeans used rifles. The Indians, whose only weapons were bows and arrows, could not compete with weaponry such as rifles and cannons. They relied on their ability to hide in the forests, something the English found troublesome.

The Indians were nomadic, traveling to find food; they did not believe in owning land. They abandoned but did not destroy the land. They respected the land as a gift from the gods. The Europeans believed in owning the land and using it to produce food — first by hand and later with the help of machines.

As the British colonies became more populated, British settlers began moving into the lands occupied by the Indians. The French, who had also arrived in the United States by this time, also began moving west. However the English and French treated the Indians very differently. The French settled among and even inter-married with them; the British continued to consider themselves superior to the Indians and wanted no part of them.

The French were concerned about what they considered encroachment of the British into the Mississippi River area and the St. Lawrence Seaway watershed, which included the Ohio River and the Great Lakes. To protect what they considered their land, they began to build forts on Lake Champlain and the Mississippi, Missouri, Wabash, and Ohio rivers.

The British joined the fort building at Oswego and Halifax and traders set up bases in the region granted to the Ohio Company by the government.

British, French Move into Ohio Valley

As expansion continued, tension between the British and French mounted. In 1750 representatives of the two countries met in Paris to try and resolve the dispute but failed. Two years later the governor of New France, Marquis Duquesne, was ordered to claim the region for his homeland and drive the British out of the Ohio Valley. In 1753 he led his troops into the western part of Pennsylvania where they established forts at Presque Isle on Lake Erie and on the Waterford River.

At the same time, Virginia Lieutenant Governor Robert Dinwiddie granted land in the area to British citizens.

The movement of the French and British into the region was the precursor of the French and Indian War. Concerned about the fort-building actions of the French, Dinwiddie sent George Washington to deliver a letter to the French on the upper Allegheny River ordering them out of the area; they refused.

Upon his return Washington suggested that the point of land where the Allegheny and Monongahela rivers combined to form the Ohio River would make an excellent location for a fort. The plan to occupy the strategic fork was formed by Dinwiddie. In January 1754 the British began to build Fort Prince George — the first of several forts that were built to control the strategic forks of the Ohio River — at the outset of the French and Indian War but they never completed the fort.

Captain William Trent was in command but when the French and Indians arrived at the fort, he had been recalled to Wills Creek for a conference and his second-in-command, Lieutenant John Fraser, was at his own Turtle Creek plantation on the Monongahela River, leaving Ensign Edward Ward in charge at the time of the surrender of Fort Prince George on April 18, 1754.

Strike Starts French and Indian War

After the French drove out the British they claimed the point of land, finished the fort, and renamed it Fort Duquesne. Hearing about the actions at the fort, Washington, who was helping the British establish control in the west, set up an encampment southeast of Fort Duquesne.

To keep the French from attacking the new camp, Washington made a pre-emptive strike on the fort — the first action of the as-yet-undeclared French and Indian War. Although successful in that strike, Washington was soon defeated by the French who claimed control of all land west of the Allegheny Mountains.

Throughout the seventeenth and eighteenth centuries, Britain and France along with the Iroquois claimed ownership of the Ohio Country. When Britain and France sent traders into the area in the mid-1700s violence erupted once again in the French and Indian War, which was settled when the Treaty of Paris was signed in 1763. France relinquished claims to the area, but the British stayed.

Northwest Territory off Limits to Settlers

In 1763 the British closed the Northwest Territory to further European settlement in an attempt to appease the Shawnee and other tribes in the region. The territory provided a safe haven for the Indians until settlers began to stretch out across their new land, moving from New England and heading toward the Ohio Territory via the Erie Canal, toward Lake Erie, and the Ohio River.

The Indian tribes, wanting the British out of the area, burned homes and killed or drove out many of the settlers between 1763 and 1766. In June 1774 the British Parliament passed the Quebec Act, making the Northwest Territory a part of Quebec.

Ohio, especially the area around the southern border of Lake Erie, was prime territory but getting there was a problem because of the Indians. In the fall of 1775, the Kentucky settlement in Ohio Country was under attack by the British and Shawnee, Cherokee, Delaware, Ottawa, Wyandot, Iroquois, and Mingo tribes.

By 1779, the settlement was almost wiped out. General George Rogers Clark with a militia of 175 men floated down the Ohio River. He arrived at the settlement February 23, 1779, and captured Kaskaskia, Cahokia, and Fort Vincennes without firing a shot, weakening the British position in the Northwest Territory. British General Henry Hamilton, who was at Fort Sackville, was unaware of the Clark expedition and unprepared to defend the forts; he surrendered two days later.

The battles between the Indians and the American settlers continued throughout the Revolutionary War with the land continually switching hands.

Franklin Signs 1783 Treaty

In 1783, the American colonists defeated the British; the thirteen colonies became the original states, which created a Congress. Benjamin Franklin was in Paris for the signing of the second Treaty of Paris in 1783. He convinced the French to side with and send troops to support the Americans. He also convinced France's King Louis XVI to finance the Americans, albeit under false pretenses, which eventually led to the French Revolution.

The treaty gave the United States authority over all land east of the Mississippi River and south of the Great Lakes — at least on paper. The territory included all the land west of Pennsylvania and northwest of the Ohio River. The British maintained their Canadian possessions and Spanish Territory in Florida.

The Indians in the Ohio Country took no formal part in the treaty negotiations. Great

Britain made little effort to include their Indian allies in the terms of the treaty but did not abandon the Indians. They continued to trade guns and other European manufactured goods for native furs. The British hoped that the Indians, armed with English weapons, would stop the westward expansion of the newly independent Americans.

After the signing of 1783 Treaty of Paris, settlers quickly moved into the Ohio Country. They faced few obstacles other than from the Indians. The Indians did not welcome the settlers who were moving into what they considered their territory. They knew that the treaties signed by the colonists had little meaning and were generally ignored; the colonists went where they pleased. The Indians watched settlers arriving by the hundreds and destroying their hunting grounds in the late 1780s and early 1790s. The conflicts that followed became known as the Ohio Indian Wars.

The tribes that were not part of the treaty agreement in 1783 refused to recognize the Americans' claim to the land.

Indians Re-activate Confederacy

Two events in 1785 had opposing effects. The Land Ordinance encouraged settlers to acquire new land from the Indians, who might or might not control the property. Congress negotiated the Treaty of Fort McIntosh with several Indian tribes. However by that time settlers from Connecticut were pouring into the Western Reserve.

The member tribal bands of the Western Confederacy consisting of several bands of Indians formed during the French Colonial Period, regrouped and re-activated the confederacy in 1785 at Fort Detroit to deal with the United States settlers as a group rather than as individual tribes. The confederacy demanded that the Ohio River be the dividing line between their lands and those of the settlers.

British agents, still angry from being ousted from land they believed was theirs, sold weapons and ammunition to the tribes and encouraged them to attack the American settlers. A series of isolated raids resulted in growing mistrust and bloodshed.

It escalated to the point Federal troops and the Kentucky Militia rode against the Shawnee in the fall of 1786. When a Shawnee chief was killed, raids on both sides of the Ohio River became more frequent.

The Northwest Ordinance of 1787, also called the Freedom Ordinance, created the first organized territory of the United States. It covered land south of the Great Lakes, north and west of the Ohio River and east of the Mississippi River; prior to that time development had been banned in the area.

Ordinance Sets Expansion Plan

The ordinance is arguably the second most important piece of legislation passed by the Continental Congress — the most important being the Declaration of Independence. It established the way the United States would expand westward: admission of new states rather than expanding existing states.

Above all, the Northwest Ordinance accelerated the westward expansion of the United States, providing for the creation of not less than three or more than five states.

It also banned slavery in the territory, effectively establishing the Ohio River as the boundary between free and slave territory in the area between the Mississippi River and the Appalachian Mountains. It set the stage for the balancing act between free and slave states that was the basis of a critical question in American politics until the Civil War. It also contained provisions for advancing education and maintaining civil liberties.

The ordinance mandated the creation of new states once the population within a particular territory reached 60,000. The legalities for admission of a new state were established in the Enabling Act of 1802; the first state created from the territory was Ohio the following year.

Maxwell's Code Establishes Laws

Brigadier General Arthur St. Clair played a major part in the settlements in that region following the Ordinance of 1787 and the settlement of the Northwest Territory. In 1788 he was appointed governor of Ohio Territory. He formulated Maxwell's Code — the first written laws of the territory — and also sought to end Indian claims to Ohio land and clear the way for white settlement.

The late 1780s pitted the whites against the Indians as the settlers moved into the territory. It fell on St. Clair's shoulders to establish peace between the two groups. In mid-December 1788, St. Clair met with representatives of some of the Indian tribes at Fort Harmer, near present-day Mariette, Ohio, to negotiate a peaceful end to the hostilities.

Representatives from the Wyandot, Delaware, Chippewa, Ottawa, Sauk, and Potawatomi were present and requested that St. Clair establish an Indian reserve on land north of the Ohio River and west of the Muskingum River.

St. Clair refused and demanded that the chiefs agree to a reservation established by the Treaty of Fort McIntosh in 1785 in which the tribes had ceded all land in Ohio Country east of to Cuyahoga and Muskingum rivers, and areas surrounding Fort Detroit and Fort Michilimackinac to the American government. The tribes also freed the captives taken in frontier raids.

New Treaty Changes Little

On January 9, 1789, representatives of the tribes signed the Treaty of Fort Harmar, but not without a little double-dealing by St. Clair. On one hand, he threatened to attack the Indians if they refused to honor the boundaries set in 1785 and on the other hand he bribed them with $3000 worth of presents.

The treaty simply re-iterated the Treaty of Fort McIntosh and settled little. Many Indian leaders had not been invited to participate in the negotiations or had refused to do so. Problems with the new treaty arose almost as soon as the ink dried.

The Connecticut Western Reserve extended west of the Cuyahoga River into the reservation lands. In 1792 Connecticut had set aside 500,000 acres land in the region, known as the Fire Lands or the Sufferers' Lands for veterans of the Revolutionary War and Patriots that had lost their homes in the war. Few of the original sufferers ever settled there because if ongoing Indian conflicts prior to and during the War of 1812. In addition, much of the land was dense forests, unsuitable for farming.

Further complicating the matter, Great Britain continued to claim part of the region and would do so until the Jay Treaty was signed in 1794. Some British agents in the region — still stinging from their defeat in the Revolution — encouraged the tribes to attack American settlements.

When St. Clair failed to improve the relations between the tribes and the settlers the bloodshed continued. Many of the Indians, including the Shawnee and Miamis, refused to honor the treaty claiming the tribes that were party to the treaty did not represent them.

Treaty provokes Indians

Instead of settling the Indians' claims, the treaty provoked them to further resistance, in what became known as the Northwest Indian War or Little Turtle's War. The war actually began in 1785 and intensified after the Treaty of Fort Harmar. It involved the United States and the Western Confederacy for control of the Northwest Territory.

In 1790, George Washington was appointed — not elected — the first president of the United States. The new United States Congress believed that Washington had the natural strength to lead the new nation because of his integrity during the American Revolution.

However, he faced a triple dilemma:

- Working with the Indians to find a solution for the peaceful settlement of lands west of the Appalachians and into the Ohio Valley. Once they had gained their independence from Britain, many Americans were eager to push westward but were uncertain about going into an area because of an expanding confederacy among Indian tribes in the area.
- Finding a way for the new country to repay the soldiers who fought for him and those who gave their lives for the new land.
- Returning thousands of acres of destroyed land to a productive state; a lesser, but still daunting, task.

Washington knew what happened to the colonists that ventured into Indian country during the French and Indian War and the American Revolution. At the urging of the governors of the colonies, he appointed special troops to engage the Indians.

Settlers on Their Own

But the United States government didn't have the money to equip an army to deal with the growing threat. And in spite of the obvious danger, Washington decided to repay the veterans by allowing them to settle west of the Appalachians with no limit on the amount of land they could obtain. However, the veteran settlers were left to defend themselves.

Secretary of War Henry Knox ordered St. Clair to establish a peaceful relationship between the settlers and the natives. This was an eventual stronghold for the American dream and westward manifest destiny for the future — if it could be secured.

The idea turned into a disaster for the settlers; they were attacked by the Indians who saw them as intruders. Entire settlements were destroyed; settlers were scalped and burned. Many fled back to the safety east of the Appalachians.

The Americans were also being challenged by the British for ownership of land around the Great Lakes. The British persuaded and supported Indian attacks against the American settlers because they still wanted to control the land west of the Mississippi River Valley. They watched with delight as the Americans were defeated by the Indians in the Ohio Valley.

Fort Pitt Becomes Army Headquarters

Washington thought he was prepared to handle this situation. He recognized what was happening because of his earlier experiences dealing with the British. He made Fort Pitt the headquarters for the American Army, which he created and commanded, in spite of a lack of funds.

From there he could disperse the soldiers to follow the Ohio River into the Virginia Military tracks in the southern most sections of Ohio. (Kentucky and Tennessee were also major American settlement areas. Following the American Revolution, the Indians seemed to be contained in these areas.)

It soon became apparent that Washington had underestimated the British, who were able to draw bands of Indians and Indian leaders — including Little Turtle — to their side with little effort. The master warrior carried great weight among not only some of the Miami tribes but also some of the Delaware, Shawnee, and Wabash tribes.

Army Starts to Force Out Indians

Beginning in 1790, on orders from the secretary of war, the American military led by Brigadier General Josiah Harmar, commander of the American Army in Ohio Territory, started to force the Indians out of Ohio Country. Harmar launched a major offensive into the Shawnee and Miami country in the Northwest Territory.

In October, Harmer left Fort Washington with 1420 men — roughly 1,100 militiamen and 320 regular soldiers. Most of the militiamen were from Kentucky and Pennsylvania. Many had little or no training in loading and firing a musket; some didn't even have a weapon. Harmar set out to destroy the villages of the Miami, Shawnee, and Delaware tribes as well as local tribes near present-day Fort Wayne, Indiana. At first he was successful, causing the Indians to flee and burning their villages.

However in October several hundred militiamen and a few army regulars under the leadership of Colonel John Harden, a Kentucky militia commander, were soundly defeated; those who weren't killed fled.

Some sources say Harden and his men were attacked by Little Turtle's men. Other sources say Hardin's party was about three-quarters of a mile from Turtle Creek when they were stopped by three or four Shawnee Indians. After learning about Hardin's mission, the Shawnee claimed to be friendly and spent the night in Hardin's camp. During the night Hardin and some of his men were murdered by their guests.

Two days later Harmer sent another contingent after Little Turtle with the same result. Following the second of what would be come a long series of losing battles with Little Turtle, Harmar retreated to the safety of Fort Washington. Following Harmar's defeat leaders of the once-reluctant Ottawa and Wyandot tribes joined the confederacy.

St. Clair Builds Forts

Washington turned to St. Clair, an inexperienced Indian fighter, but someone who Washington believed had excellent ideas on how to control the Indians. He ordered St. Clair to mount a vigorous campaign in the summer of 1791 but that was doomed from the start. St. Clair had trouble finding men and supplies and the men he did find received little training.

St. Clair led an attack against the Miami, Shawnee, and Delaware villages near modern-day Fort Wayne, Indiana, with two regular army regiments and militiamen from Kentucky and some of the original 13 states.

In September 1791 St. Clair began building a chain of forts 25 miles apart all the way up the Ohio River, and moved north with about 2000 men erecting Fort Hamilton and Fort Jefferson.

By November 3, 1791, when he reached the Wabash River the army was down to 1400 men. The majority of the unruly militiamen who did not respect or like him had deserted.

He had weak perimeter defenses and before sunrise November 4 was surprised and quickly surrounded by 2000 Indians led by Blue Jacket, Tecumseh, and Little Turtle. Half of St. Clair's men were killed before noon and the remainder ran leaving everything behind — bodies, cannons, muskets, horses, and wagons. They retreated to the safety of Fort Jefferson, which they had built about a month earlier.

Little Turtle lost fewer than two dozen men. The American Army lost about 69 percent of its troops, making St. Clair's Massacre — also referred to as the Battle of the Wabash — the greatest defeat of the United States Army by Indian forces.

St. Clair's pounding at the hands of Little Turtle and Blue Jacket in the Battle of the Wabash, ended his military career and prompted Congress to undertake a full investigation of the loss.

Between 1790 and 1794, the British convinced the Indians to battle the American settlers for control of the land. Little Turtle gained control of the Ohio Territory and assembled about 2000 braves while Washington failed at every turn. The tide wouldn't turn until the Battle of Fallen Timbers in 1794

Chapter Three
Tide Begins to Change

Washington calls for Wayne's Help

The eyes of the world were on the Northwest Territory during the 1790s. Wayne's actions and leadership skills played a key role in the successful westward movement in the Northwest Territory.

Britain still hoped to regain the territory it once owned; Spain had its eye on the trans-Alleghany West; and France had become more and more interested in establishing its own empire in America.

The situation in the Northwest Territory was becoming a national embarrassment to Washington because he knew that the Miami Indians and their federation were backed by the British.

Following St. Clair's embarrassing defeat on the banks of the Wabash in 1791, the credibility of the government was in shambles. Meanwhile, the Americans began to worry that a military confrontation would lead to another war against the British.

Negotiations were no more successful than the battlefield campaigns in the Northwest Territory War. The Indians refused to allow the American "intruders" to settle on what they believed was their land and the United States refused to keep its citizens east of the Ohio River.

Boundary Negotiations Fail

American settlers were already moving into the Ohio Territory, land they had claimed from Great Britain after American Revolution.

However, Shawnee war chief Blue Jacket and Delaware (Lenape) leader Buckongahelas, encouraged by their recent victories over United States troops and the hope of continued British support, pressed for the Ohio River boundary line established with Britain by the Treaty of Fort Stanwix, present-day Rome, New York, November 5, 1768.

That treaty came about because the westward push of population and economic growth turned the attention of investors and land speculators to the lands west of the Appalachians. That treaty adjusted the boundary between Indian and British land farther to the west.

The British hoped a new boundary might end the frontier violence, which had become both costly and disquieting. The Indians hoped a new permanent line would stop colonial expansion by the British.

The new boundary was shifted much farther to the west. It ran near Fort Pitt and followed the Ohio River as far as the Tennessee River. It ceded the Kentucky portion of the Colony of Virginia as well as most of present-day West Virginia to the Indians.

The Indians rejected the subsequent treaties that ceded lands north of the Ohio River to the United States.

A faction led by the influential Mohawk leader Joseph Brant attempted to negotiate a compromise, but Blue Jacket and his allies would accept nothing less than an Ohio River boundary, which the United States refused.

Washington Organizes Legion

Washington sent for Wayne, who had established himself as "a true Indian fighter." He named him commanding general of the Legion of the United States, the brain child of Secretary of War Knox, to lead an expedition into the Northwest Indian Territory.

The Legion was recruited and re-organized in Pittsburg, Pennsylvania. Units of the old 1st and 2nd regiments became the 1st and 2nd sub-legions. From June 1792 to November 1792 the army was lodged at Fort LaFayette, in Pittsburg.

In October Wayne scoured the Ohio River for a suitable wintering and training spot for the Legion away from distractions of the city. He found what he was looking for 22 miles from Pittsburgh on the west bank of the river at what today is Baden, Pennsylvania, near Logstown, a former Indian village from about 1725 to 1758.

On November 28, 1792, Wayne and his men left Fort LaFayette with the good wishes of the Pittsburgh residents; four hours later they were at the new encampment that Wayne named Legion Ville (today spelled Legionville), the first formal United States military basic training facility.

Work was already under way by an advance group that arrived November 9. By December Legion Ville had more than 500 buildings and was four times bigger than Pittsburgh.

The east-west camp had ravines on the north, east and west. It was ringed by four fortifications; a ditch around the housing area was more than a mile long. Each fort area served as a garrison for 36 men; an additional 120 were stationed around the perimeter. The camp was guarded by 260 men, 24 hours a day, seven days a week.

The enlisted men of the dragoons, infantry, artillery and rifle-corps were housed in single-story huts; officers of the dragoons and artillery had two-story barracks. Wayne's house and the hospital were two-story log cabins with chimneys on both sides. The winter military encampment covered roughly 35 acres; estimates of the personnel vary but 2500 seems to be the most common estimate from various sources.

Wayne Orders Rigorous Training

Wayne believed the previous expeditions had failed because of the poor training and discipline. That was about to change because he had time to train his new army while peace negotiations were under way during the summer of 1793.

The cavalry led byCapt. Robert M. Campbell built an obstacle course south of Legion Ville. The artillery lieutenants and captains built an artillery range. An auxiliary rifle range was built a half-mile west of the site.

Wayne wanted trained marksmen when he attacked. As soon as the encampment was ready he began rigorous preparations. Troops had daily target practice. Bayonet drills, hand-to-hand combat, mock battles, and overnight encampments outside camp were common.

Troops marched continually with emphasis on battle formations and tactics, especially for the new officers. Wayne trained some of his disciplined regulars to be tough enough to back the skittish military.

Disobedience wasn't tolerated; minor infractions earned the soldier a lashing with a Cat-o-Nine Tails; court-martials were common. Captain William Eaton, who would eventually lead the U.S. Marines ashore at Tripoli in 1806, was often the presiding judge.

During the winter sixteen additional soldiers died and were buried in an unmarked cemetery. (Historians and archaeologists are still trying to determine the exact location.)

Campaign Begins in Spring

When spring arrived and the Indians still showed no sign of being interested in peace, Washington gave the go-ahead for the campaign. On April 30, 1793, the largest flotilla of military barges ever assembled on the Ohio River left Legion Ville for Fort Washington, Cincinnati, Ohio.

Always known for being impetuous, Wayne stepped out of character and settled at Fort Jefferson, seventy-five miles north of Cincinnati to wait for spring when he planned to launch his attack.

The unit combined all land combat arms (cavalry, infantry, and artillery) into a single efficient brigade-size, well-trained force that could be divided into stand-alone units as the situation demanded.

Wayne built a frontier fort in western Pennsylvania. After Christmas 1793 he took a small group into Indian country where they constructed Fort Recovery (now called Fort Recovery, Ohio) on the site of St. Clair's catastrophic pounding two years earlier. The fort was complete in March 1794.

Wayne Wants to Make Point

Wayne purposely chose the location because he wanted to demonstrate that the Legion of the United States could recover from St. Clair's crushing defeat and emerge victorious in Little Turtle's War, aka the Northwest Indian War. It would later be a reference point for the boundary line established in the 1795 Treaty of Greenville.

On June 30, 1794, a supply column left Fort Recovery for Fort Green Ville, another pioneer fort built under Wayne's command. Major William McMahon led the group escorted by ninety riflemen under Captain Asa Hartshome and fifty dragoons under Lieutenant Edmund Taylor.

They were less than a quarter of a mile from the fort when they were attacked by Indians commanded by Blue Jacket and a young Tecumseh. The Americans returned to the fort immediately but 32 men were killed and 30 more wounded.

During the night, a scouting company was led by Captain William Wells, the son-on-law of Little Turtle who originally fought with the Miamis but switched to the American side during the course of the Northwest Indian War with the permission of Little Turtle. He reported British officers with powder and cannonballs, but no cannons, were behind the Indian lines.

The British were looking for U.S. cannons that had been buried after St. Clair's defeat, not knowing that they had already been recovered by the Legion of the United States.

Defeat Shakes Indians' Confidence

The following day the Indian forces attacked the fort again, but began to withdraw by noon and were gone by nightfall. Following the defeat, the Indians confidence was shaken.

Wayne also set up forts all along the way as he headed north and staffed these forts with trained Legionnaires to ensure adequate re-supply points.

He constructed Fort Defiance, present day Defiance, Ohio, in August 1794 at the confluence of the Auglaize and Maumee Rivers to protect his men and as a staging area for operations against the Indians of Ohio.

The fort was a rough square with a blockhouse on each corner. In addition to the stockade, an earthen wall, eight-feet thick and a ditch eight-feet deep and fifteen-feet wide, protected the fortifications. Lieutenant John Boyer, an officer in Wayne's army, claimed that the fort could protect the American soldiers from "the English, the Indians, and all the devils in hell."

The fort served as one of the western-most outposts in Ohio, guarding against attacks by Indians until the War of 1812.

Wayne moves deeper

By the fall of 1794, Wayne moved deeper into Indian-held territory near Maumee Rapids. He commanded about 4600 men and used Choctaw and Chickasaw Indians as scouts.

Blue Jacket's army took a defensive stand along the Maumee River in present-day Maumee, Ohio, and not far from present-day Toledo, Ohio, where a stand of trees had blown down ("fallen timbers") by a tornado or heavy storm. They believed that the trees would hinder the advance of the army.

Fort Miami, a nearby British outpost supplied provisions for the Indian confederacy. The Indian army of about 1500 men, consisted of Blue Jacket's Shawnees and Buckongahelas's Delawares, Miamis led by Little Turtle, Wyandots, Ojibwas, Ottawas, Potawatomis, Mingos, and even some Canadian militia.

At the Battle of Fallen Timbers on August 20, 1794, Wayne's troops defeated a British-supported force of Indians led by Little Turtle in less than an hour. When Wayne's troops arrived many of Little Turtle's men were gathering supplies from the British stronghold at Fort Miami. Those who remained were outflanked by the Legion Cavalry.

The Indians retreated to Fort Miami only to find the gates locked. The British commander at the fort was not authorized to start a war with the Americans and refused to allow the Indians to enter.

The American troops destroyed Indian villages and crops in the area and then withdrew with 33 killed and another 100 wounded. The number of Indian casualties varies according to the source ranging from 19 to 40.

Today a small park near the battle site includes a monument in honor of Wayne and other monuments to the soldiers and Indians who died in the battle. The park near Maumee, Ohio, is maintained by the Ohio Historical Society. On September 14th, 1929 the U.S. Post office issued a stamp commemorating the 150th anniversary of the Battle of Fallen Timbers.

Victory Settles Ownership

Wayne's victory over the Indian Confederacy ended the 10-year Northwest Indian War and the power of the British on American soil. Following the defeat of their Indian allies, the British evacuated U.S. forts that they had occupied in defiance of the Treaty of Paris (1783).

The Battle of Fallen Timbers, which took place about 15 miles southwest of present day Toledo, Ohio, settled the ownership of the Northwest Territory — an area bordered by the Great Lakes on the northeast, the Ohio River on the south and the Mississippi River on the west.

The decisive victory for the federal troops ended the hostilities with the Indians until the Battle of Tippecanoe in 1811 and Tecumseh's War between the American Indian Confederacy led by Tecumseh, and the federal troops.

Chapter Four
Both Sides Sign Treaty

Much of Ohio, Indiana Opens to Settlement

The victory was the primary impetus leading to the Treaty of Greenville signed on August 3, 1795, at Fort Greenville (present day Greenville, Ohio) putting an end to the Northwest Indian War. The treaty between the Western Confederacy, and the United States was signed almost a decade after the Revolutionary War.

As a result of the treaty, the Indians ceded most of Ohio and much of Indiana, opening the area to settlement.

The treaty established the "Greenville Treaty Line," which was a boundary between Indian Territory and land open to white settlers for several years.

However the treaty line was frequently disregarded by settlers as they continued to encroach on lands given to the Indians under the treaty.

Wayne represented the United States, which agreed to pay the equivalent of $20,000 in goods and services (domestic animals, blankets, cooking utensils, etc.) to the Indians.

In exchange representatives of several bands of the Wyandot, Delaware, Shawnee, Ottawa, Chippewa, Potawatomi, Miami, Wea, Kickapoo, and Kaskaskia Indians gave the United States the Fort Detroit area, the future site of Chicago and large parts of Ohio.

Under the terms of the treaty:

- The tribes agreed to surrender their claims to lands in the southeastern portion of the Northwest Territory — primarily present-day southern and eastern Ohio.
- The tribes also gave up additional defined areas that were used by the whites as portages and fort locations. This category included Fort Detroit and the future site Chicago.
- In additional to the initial payment the U.S. government agreed to annual payments of $9,500 in goods to be divided among specified tribes
- The tribes retained the right to hunt throughout the area.

Once again, the Americans ignored the terms and began establishing new settlements almost as soon as the treaty was signed.

The Indians, on the other hand, followed the treaty to the letter. More trouble would break out farther to the west in the next century under the leadership of Tecumseh and his brother, The Prophet.

A Treaty of Peace

BETWEEN THE

UNITED STATES OF AMERICA

AND THE

TRIBES OF INDIANS,

CALLED THE

Wyandots, Delawares, Shawanoes, Ottawas, Chipewas, Putawatimes, Miamis, Eel-river, Weeás, Kickapoos, Pian-kaſhaws, and Kaſkaſkias.

TO put an end to a deſtructive war, to ſettle all controverſies, and to reſtore harmony and a friendly intercourſe between the ſaid United States, and Indian tribes ; Anthony Wayne, major-general, commanding the army of the United States, and ſole commiſſioner for the good purpoſes above-mentioned, and the ſaid tribes of Indians, by their Sachems, chiefs, and warriors, met together at Greeneville, the head quarters of the ſaid army, have agreed on the following articles, which, when ratified by the Preſident, with the advice and conſent of the Senate of the United States, ſhall be binding on them and the ſaid Indian tribes.

ARTICLE I.

Henceforth all hoſtilities ſhall ceaſe ; peace is hereby eſtabliſhed, and ſhall be perpetual ; and a friendly intercourſe ſhall take place, between the ſaid United States and Indian tribes.

Peace eſtabliſhed

ARTICLE II.

All priſoners ſhall on both ſides be reſtored. The Indians, priſoners to the United States, ſhall be immediately ſet at liberty. The peo-

Vol. II.   L 3

Cover of Treaty of Greenville

Treaty of Greenville

(Reprinted from an original. Punctuation and spelling are in the style of the original document.)

A treaty of peace between the United States of America and the tribes of Indians called the Wyandots, Delawares, Shawanoes, Ottawas, Chipewas, Putawatimes, Miamis, Eel-river, Weeas, Kickapoos, Piankashaws and Kaskaskias.

(Signed on August 3, 1795, at Fort Greenville.)

To put an end to a destructive war, to settle all controversies, and to restore harmony and friendly intercourse between the said United States and Indian tribes, Anthony Wayne, major general commanding the army of the United States, and sole commissioner for the good purposes above mentioned, and the said tribes of Indians, by their sachems, chiefs, and warriors, met together at Greenville, the head quarters of the said army, have agreed on the following articles, which, when ratified by the President, with the advice and consent of the Senate of the United States, shall be binding on them and the said Indian tribes.

Article I
Henceforth all hostilities shall cease; peace is hereby established, and shall be perpetual; and a friendly intercourse shall take place between the said United States and Indian tribes.

Article II
All prisoners shall, on both sides, be restored. The Indians, prisoners to the United States, shall be immediately set at liberty. The people of the United States, still remaining prisoners among the Indians, shall be delivered up in ninety days from the date hereof, to the general or commanding officer at Greeneville, Fort Wayne, or Fort

Defiance; and ten chiefs of the said tribes shall remain at Greeneville as hostages, until the delivery of the prisoners shall be effected.

Article III

The general boundary line between the lands of the United States and the lands of the said Indian tribes, shall begin at the mouth of Cayahoga river, and run thence up the same to the portage, between that and the Tuscarawas branch of the Muskingum, thence down that branch to the crossing place above Fort Lawrence, thence westerly to a fork of that branch of the Great Miami river, running into the Ohio, at or near which fork stood Loromie's store, and where commences the portage between the Miami of the Ohio, and St. Mary's river, which is a branch of the Miami which runs into lake Erie; thence a westerly course to Fort Recovery, which stands on a branch of the Wabash; thence south-westerly in a direct line to the Ohio, so as to intersect that river opposite the mouth of Kentucke or Cuttawa river. And in consideration of the peace now established; of the goods formerly received from the United States; of those now to be delivered; and of the yearly delivery of goods now stipulated to be made hereafter; and to indemnify the United States for the injuries and expenses they have sustained during the war, the said Indian tribes do hereby cede and relinquish forever, all their claims to the lands lying eastwardly and southwardly of the general boundary line now described: and these lands, or any part of them, shall never hereafter be made a cause or pretence, on the part of the said tribes, or any of them, of war or injury to the United States, or any of the people thereof. And for the same considerations, and as an evidence of the returning friendship of the said Indian tribes, of their confidence in the United States, and desire to provide for their accommodations, and for that convenient intercourse which will be beneficial to both parties, the said Indian tribes do also cede to the United States the following pieces of land, to wit: (1) One piece of land six miles square, at or near Loromie's store, before mentioned. (2) One piece two miles square, at the head of the navigable water or landing, on the St. Mary's river, near Girty's town. (3) One piece six miles square, at the head of the navigable water of the Auglaize river. (4) One piece six miles square, at the confluence of the Auglaize and Miami rivers, where Fort Defiance now stands. (5) One piece six miles square, at or near the confluence of the rivers St. Mary's and St. Joseph's, where Fort Wayne now stands, or near it. (6) One piece two miles square, on the Wabash river, at the end of the portage from the Miami of the lake, and about eight miles westward from Fort Wayne. (7) One piece six miles square, at the Ouatanon, or Old Wea towns, on the Wabash river. (8) One piece twelve miles square, at the British fort on the Miami of the lake, at the foot of the rapids. (9) One piece six miles square, at the mouth of the said river, where it empties into the lake. (10) One piece six miles square, upon Sandusky lake, where a fort formerly stood. (11) One piece two miles square, at the lower rapids of Sandusky river. (12) The post of Detroit, and all the land to the north, the west and the south of it, of which the Indian title has been extinguished by gifts or grants to the French or English governments: and so much more land to be annexed to the district of Detroit, as shall be comprehended between the river Rosine, on the south, Lake St. Clair on the north, and a line, the general course whereof shall be six miles distant from the west end of lake Erie and Detroit river. (13) The post of Michilimackinac, and all the land on the island on which that post stands, and the main land adjacent, of which the Indian title has been extinguished by gifts or grants to the French or English governments; and a piece of land on the main to the north of the island, to measure six miles, on Lake Huron, or the strait between lakes Huron and Michigan, and to extend three miles back from the water of the lake or strait; and also, the Island De Bois Blane, being an extra and voluntary gift of the Chippewa nation. (14) One piece of land six miles square, at the mouth of Chikagoriver, emptying into the southwest end of Lake Michigan, where a fort formerly stood. (15) One piece twelve miles square, at or near the mouth of the Illinois river, emptying into the Mississippi. (16) One piece six miles square, at the old Piorias fort and village near the south end of the Illinois lake, on said Illinois river. And whenever the United States shall think proper to survey and mark the boundaries of the lands hereby ceded to them, they shall give timely notice thereof to the said tribes of Indians that they may appoint some of their wise chiefs to attend and see that the lines are run according to the terms of this treaty. And the said Indian tribes will allow to the people of the United States a free passage by land and by water, as one and the other shall be found convenient, through their country, along the chain of posts herein-before mentioned; that is to say, from the commencement of the portage aforesaid, at or near Loromie's store, thence along said portage to the St. Mary's, and down the same to fort Wayne, and then down the Miami, to lake Erie; again, from the commencement of the portage at or near Loromie's store along the portage from thence to the river Auglaize, and down the same to its junction with the Miami at fort Defiance; again, from the commencement of the portage aforesaid, to Sandusky river, and down the same to Sandusky bay and lake Erie, and from Sandusky to the post which shall be taken at or near the foot of the Rapids of the Miami of the lake; and from thence to Detroit. Again, from the mouth of Chikago, to the commencement of the portage, between that river and the Illinois, and down the Illinois river to the Mississippi; also, from Fort Wayne, along the portage aforesaid, which leads to the Wabash, and then down the Wabash to the Ohio. And the said Indian tribes will also allow to the people of the United States, the free use of the harbors and mouths of rivers along the lakes adjoining the Indian lands, for sheltering vessels and boats, and liberty to land their cargoes where necessary for their safety.

Article IV

In consideration of the peace now established, and of the cessions and relinquishment of lands made in the preceding article by the said tribes of Indians, and to manifest the liberality of the United States, as the great means of rendering this peace strong and perpetual, the United States relinquish their claims to all other Indian lands northward of the river Ohio, eastward of the Mississippi, and westward and southward of the Great Lakes and the waters, uniting them, according to the boundary line agreed on by the United States and the King of Great Britain, in the treaty of peace made between them in the year 1783. But from this relinquishment by the United States, the following tracts of land are explicitly excepted: 1st. The tract on one hundred and fifty thousand acres near the rapids of the river Ohio, which has been assigned to General Clark, for the use of himself and his warriors. 2nd. The post of St. Vincennes, on the River Wabash, and the lands adjacent, of which the Indian title has been extinguished. 3rd. The lands at all other places in possession of the French people and other white settlers among them, of which the Indian title has been extinguished as mentioned in the 3d article; and 4th. The post of fort Massac towards the mouth of the Ohio. To which several parcels of land so excepted, the said tribes relinquish all the title and claim which they or any of them may have. And for the same considerations and with the same views as above mentioned, the United States now deliver to the said Indian tribes a quantity of goods to the value of twenty thousand dollars, the receipt whereof they do hereby acknowledge; and henceforward every year, forever, the United States will deliver, at some convenient place northward of the river Ohio, like useful goods, suited to the circumstances of the Indians, of the value of nine thousand five hundred dollars; reckoning that value at the first cost of the goods in the city or place in the United States where they shall be procured. The tribes to which those goods are to be annually delivered, and the proportions in which they are to be delivered, are the following: 1st. To the Wyandots, the amount of one thousand dollars. 2nd. To the Delawares, the amount of one thousand dollars. 3rd. To the Shawanees, the amount of one thousand dollars. 4th. To the Miamis, the amount of one thousand dollars. 5th. To the Ottawas, the amount of one thousand dollars. 6th. To the Chippewas, the amount of one thousand dollars. 7th. To the Pattawatimas, the amount of one thousand dollars, and 8th. To the Kickapoo, Wea, Eel River, Piankeshaw, and Kaskaskia tribes, the amount of five hundred dollars each. Provided, that if either of the said tribes shall hereafter, at an annual delivery of their share of the goods aforesaid, desire that a part of their annuity should be furnished in domestic animals, implements of husbandry, and other utensils convenient for them, and in compensation to useful artificers who may reside with or near them, and be employed for their benefit, the same shall, at the subsequent annual deliveries, be furnished accordingly.

Article V

To prevent any misunderstanding about the Indian lands relinquished by the United States in the fourth article, it is now explicitly declared, that the meaning of that relinquishment is this: the Indian tribes who have a right to those lands, are quietly to enjoy them, hunting, planting, and dwelling thereon, so long as they please, without any molestation from the United States; but when those tribes, or any of them, shall be disposed to sell their lands, or any part of them, they are to be sold only to the United States; and until such sale, the United States will protect all the said Indian tribes in the quiet enjoyment of their lands against all citizens of the United States, and against all other white persons who intrude upon the same. And the said Indian tribes again acknowledge themselves to be under the protection of the said United States, and no other power whatever.

Article VI

If any citizen of the United States, or any other white person or persons, shall presume to settle upon the lands now relinquished by the United States, such citizen or other person shall be out of the protection of the United States; and the Indian tribe, on whose land the settlement shall be made, may drive off the settler, or punish him in such manner as they shall think fit; and because such settlements, made without the consent of the United States, will be injurious to them as well as to the Indians, the United States shall be at liberty to break them up, and remove and punish the settlers as they shall think proper, and so effect that protection of the Indian lands herein before stipulated.

Article VII

The said tribes of Indians, parties to this treaty, shall be at liberty to hunt within the territory and lands which they have now ceded to the United States, without hindrance or molestation, so long as they demean themselves peaceably, and offer no injury to the people of the United States.

Article VIII

Trade shall be opened with the said Indian tribes; and they do hereby respectively engage to afford protection to such persons, with their property, as shall be duly licensed to reside among them for the purpose of trade; and to their agents and servants; but no person shall be permitted to reside among them for the purpose of trade; and to their agents and servants; but no person shall be permitted to reside at any of their towns or hunting camps, as a trader, who is not furnished with a license for that purpose, under the hand and seal of the superintendent of the department northwest of the Ohio, or such other person as the President of the United States shall authorize to grant such licenses; to the end, that the said Indians may not be imposed on in their trade. And if any licensed trader shall abuse his privilege by unfair dealing, upon complaint and proof thereof, his license shall be taken from him, and he shall be further punished according to the laws of the United States. And if any person shall intrude himself as a trader, without such license, the said Indians shall take and bring him before the superintendent, or his deputy, to be dealt with according to law. And to prevent impositions by forged licenses, the said Indians shall, at least once a year, give information to the superintendent, or his deputies, on the names of the traders residing among them.

Article IX

Lest the firm peace and friendship now established, should be interrupted by the misconduct of individuals, the United States, and the said Indian tribes agree, that for injuries done by individuals on either side, no private revenge or retaliation shall take place; but instead thereof, complaint shall be made by the party injured, to the other: by the said Indian tribes or any of them, to the President of the United States, or the superintendent by him appointed; and by the superintendent or other person appointed by the President, to the principal chiefs of the said Indian tribes, or of the tribe to which the offender belongs; and such prudent measures shall then be taken as shall be necessary to preserve the said peace and friendship unbroken, until the legislature (or great council) of the United States, shall make other equitable provision in the case, to the satisfaction of both parties. Should any Indian tribes meditate a war against the United States, or either of them, and the same shall come to the knowledge of the before-mentioned tribes, or either of them, they do hereby engage to give immediate notice thereof to the general, or officer commanding the troops of the United States, at the nearest post.

And should any tribe, with hostile intentions against the United States, or either of them, attempt to pass through their country, they will endeavor to prevent the same, and in like manner give information of such attempt, to the general, or officer commanding, as soon as possible, that all causes of mistrust and suspicion may be avoided between them and the United States. In like manner, the United States shall give notice to the said Indian tribes of any harm that may be meditated against them, or either of them, that shall come to their knowledge; and do all in their power to hinder and prevent the same, that the friendship between them may be uninterrupted.

Article X

All other treaties heretofore made between the United States, and the said Indian tribes, or any of them, since the treaty of 1783, between the United States and Great Britain, that come within the purview of this treaty, shall henceforth cease and become void.

In testimony whereof, the said Anthony Wayne, and the sachems and war chiefs of the before-mentioned nations and tribes of Indians, have hereunto set their hands and affixed their Seals.

Done at Greeneville, in the territory of the United States north-west of the river Ohio, on the third Day of August, one thousand seven hundred and ninety-five.

Wyandots:

Tarhe, or Crane, his x mark L.S.; J. Williams, jun. his x mark, L.S.; Teyyaghtaw, his x mark, L.S.; Haroenyou, (or half king's son), his x mark, L.S.; Tehaawtorens, his x mark, L.S.; Awmeyeeray, his x mark, L.S.; Stayetah, his x mark L.S.; Shateyyaronyah, or (Leather Lips), his x mark, L.S.;

Daughshuttayah, his x mark L.S. ; Shaawrunthe, his x mark L.S.

Delawares

Tetabokshke (or Grand Glaize King), his x mark,

L.S.; Lemantanquis (or Black King), is x mark, L.S.; ;

Wabatthoe, his x mark, L.S.; Maghpiway, (or Red Feather), his x mark, L.S.; Kikthawenund, (or Anderson), his x mark, L.S.; Bukongehelas, his x mark, L.S.; Peekeelund, his x mark, L.S.; Wellebawkeelund, his x mark, L.S.; Peekeetelemund, (or Thomas Adams), his x mark, L.S.;

Kishkopekund, (or Captain Buffalo), his x mark, L.S.; Amenahehan, (or Captain Crow), his x mark, L.S. ;

Queshawksey, (or George Washington), his x mark, L.S.; Weywinquis, (or Billy Siscomb), his x mark, L.S.; Moses, his x mark, L.S.

Shawanoes

Misquacoonacaw, (or Red Pole), his x mark, L.S.; Cutthewekasaw, (or Black Hoof), his x mark, L.S.;

Kaysewaesekah, his x mark, L.S.; Weythapamattha, his x mark, L.S.; Nianysmeka, his x mark, L.S.; Waytheah, (or Long Shanks), his x mark, L.S.; Weyapiersenwaw, (or Blue Jacket), his x mark, L.S.; Nequetaughaw, his x mark, L.S.; Hahgoosekaw, (or Captain Reed), his x mark, L.S

Ottawas

ugooshaway, his x mark, L.S.; Keenoshameek, his x mark, L.S.; La Malice, his x mark, L.S.;

Machiwetah, his x mark, L.S.; Thowonawa, his x mark, L.S.; Secaw, his x mark, L.S.

Chippewas

Mashipinashiwish, (or Bad Bird), his x mark, L.S.; Nahshogashe, (from Lake Superior), his x mark, L.S.;

Kathawasung, his x mark, L.S.; Masass, his x mark, L.S.; Nemekass, (or Little Thunder), his x mark, L.S.;

Peshawkay, (or Young Ox), his x mark, L.S.; Nanguey, his x mark, L.S.; Meenedohgeesogh, his x mark, L.S.; Peewanshemenogh, his x mark, L.S.; Weymegwas, his x mark, L.S.; Gobmaatick, his x mark, L.S.

Ottawa

Chegonickska, an Ottawa from Sandusky, his x mark, L.S.; Wacheness, for himself and brother

Putawatimes of ohe River St. Joseph

Thupenebu, his x mark, L.S.; Nawac, for himself and brother Etsimethe, his x mark, L.S.; Nenanseka, his x mark, L.S.; Keesass, or Run, his x mark, L.S.; Kabamasaw, for himself and brother Chisaugan, his x mark, L.S.; Sugganunk, his x mark, L.S.; Wapmeme, (or White Pigeon), his x mark, L.S.;

Pedagoshok, his x mark, L.S.; Wabshicawnaw, his x mark, L.S.; La Chasse, his x mark, L.S.;

Meshegethenogh, for himself and brother, Wawasek, his x mark, L.S.; Hingoswash, his x mark, L.S.;

Anewasaw, his x mark, L.S.; Nawbudgh, his x mark, L.S.; Missenogomaw, his x mark, L.S.; Waweegshe, his x mark, L.S.; Thawme, or Le Blanc, his x mark, L.S.; Geeque, for himself and brother Shewinse, his x mark, L.S.

Patawatames of Huron

Okia, his x mark, L.S.; Chamung, his x mark, L.S.; Segagewan, his x mark, L.S.; Nanawme, for himself and brother A. Gin, his x mark, L.S.; Marchand, his x mark, L.S.; Wenameac, his x mark, L.S.

Miamies

Nagohquangogh, (or Le Gris), his x mark, L.S.; Meshekunnoghquoh, (or Little Turtle), his x mark, L.S

Miamis and Eel River

Peejeewa, (or Richard Ville), his x mark,; L.S. Cochkepoghtogh, his x mark, L.S,; Acoolatha, (or Little Fox), his x mark, L.S.; Francis, his x mark, L.S.

Kickapoos and Kaskaskias

Keeawhah, his x mark, L.S.; Nemighka, (or Josey Renard), his x mark, L.S.; Paikeekanogh, his x mark, L.S.; Hawkinpumiska, his x mark, L.S.; Peyamawksey, his x mark, L.S.; Reyntueco, (of the Six Nations, living at Sandusky), his x mark, L.S.

(United States — identifier inserted by author.)

H. De Butts, first A.D.C. and Sec'y to Major Gen. Wayne,; Wm. H. Harrison, Aid de Camp to Major Gen. Wayne,; T. Lewis, Aid de Camp to Major Gen. Wayne,' James O'Hara, Quartermaster Gen'l.; John Mills, Major of Infantry, and Adj. Gen'l.; Caleb Swan, P.M.T.U.S.; Gen. Demter, Lieut. Artillery; Vigo, P. Frs. La Fontaine, Ast. Lasselle, Sworn interpreters; H. Lasselle; Wm. Wells, Js.; Beau Bien,; Jacques Lasselle

David Jones, Chaplain U.S.; S. M. Morins; Lewis Beaufait; Bt. Sans Crainte; R. Lachambre; Christopher Miller; Jas. Pepen; Robert Wilson; Baties Coutien; Abraham Williams, his x mark; P. Navarre; Isaac Zane, his x mark.

(Source: The Laws of the United States of America, printed by Richard Folwell, Philadelphia, 1796.)

Chapter Five
After Fallen Timbers

Wayne Has Two Graves

Following Wayne's victory at the Battle of Fallen Timbers, he returned to a hero's welcome in Philadelphia. But Wayne was a military man of action and in June 1796 he was on the frontier overseeing the surrender of British forts to the United States.

In November he became ill with gout and died December 15, 1796, while returning to Pennsylvania from a military post in Detroit. In accordance with his wishes he was buried in a plain wood casket near Erie, Pennsylvania.

His son Isaac Wayne had other ideas and in 1809 he moved his father's remains to the family plot at St. David's Church in Radnor, Indiana. He asked Dr. J.G. Wallace who had been at the Battle of Fallen Timbers with his General Wayne to help him with the move.

When the men found the body, there was little decay. They decided it wasn't practical to cut the body into small pieces that would fit in boxes in the back of the sulky Isaac had used for the trip. Doctor Wallace dissected the body and boiled the parts to separate the flesh from the bone. The flesh was returned to the grave along with the knives used in the operation. Isaac returned to Indiana with the cleaned skeleton.

Folklore says that some of Wayne's bones came out of the boxes on the trip and that every January 1, his ghost haunts the route.

Indians Relinquish Land

During the next half century the Miamis and Algonquins gradually gave up all of their land. Negotiators for the Miami Nation and the U.S. government met at the Forks of the Wabash, near present-day Huntington, Indiana, in 1833 and again in 1840 and worked out three treaties. Events that unfolded during that time were primarily the work of two civil chiefs, Peshewa (Jean Baptiste Richardville, 1816-1841) and his son-in-law, Topeah (Francis La Fontaine, 1841-1847)

In 1818, Peshewa signed the Treaty of St. Mary, which punished the Miamis for non-support during the War of 1812. The Miamis lost most of Indiana through that treaty but Peshewa negotiated legal land grants to individual Miami families and offered his own land as a refuge for the Miamis. His actions allowed half of the Miamis to remain in Indiana when the tribes were officially moved to Oklahoma in 1846, five years after his death.

After signing the Treaty of Mississinwas in 1826, Peshewa lived in the Fort Wayne, Indiana. The federal government donated $600 to the building, which was a stipulation of the treaty. Peshewa used his own funds toward the house, and in 1827 it became the first Greek revival house in Indiana. Peshewa is considered to have been the richest man in Indiana at the time of his death in 1841. Some sources say he is buried on the grounds of Immaculate Conception Cathedral in Fort Wayne.

United States Gets More Land

By the 1826 treaty, the Miami leadership agreed to give the United States the bulk of Miami reservation lands remaining in Indiana. The families of Peshewa and certain other Miami notables were given Indiana houses and livestock furnished at government expense. The federal government agreed to buy out some of the estates granted by the previous Treaty of St. Mary's.

Small reservations were to be carved out along the Eel and Maumee rivers. The tribe was also to receive $31,040.53 — $10,000 of this in silver, the first year; and the remainder in goods the next.

The Indians were also promised a $15,000 annuity thereafter, in addition to funds provided for by other treaties. Each year $2,000 was to be set aside for the "…poor infirm persons of the Miami tribe, and for the education of the youth of the tribe as long as the Congress should …think proper…" Hunting rights would continue to be enjoyed "…so long as the same shall be the property of the United States."

However several of the government's obligations were conditional on the will of Congress. No such language limited Indian obligations, giving the Miamis a distinct disadvantage. The United States, after a vote in Congress, could walk away from some of its obligations without breaking the treaty; the Indians could not. Since most of the land in Indiana was soon parceled out to settlers, there was little open hunting ground remaining for the Miamis.

While the promises to the Miami elite seem, for the most part, to have been honored, the provisions for the maintenance of the lower orders were later modified to their detriment or ignored.

The majority of the Miami tribe was left helpless in the face of the Indian Removal Act of 1830, which paved the way for the reluctant and often forcible emigration of tens of thousands of Indians so the West. The Miamis were often at the mercy of agents from the Bureau of Indian Affairs, for whom the best interests of Indians were not always a priority.

Following Peshewa's death Topeah became the last principal chief of the Miamis and ruled over the forced split into the Western and Eastern Miami tribes in 1846. Topeah managed to keep about half of the tribe in Indiana, while the rest were sent to Kansas. Topeah accompanied the tribe members in the move west and died en route home in 1847. He is buried in Huntington.

Appendix I
Wayne's Roots

Wayne before American Revolution

Anthony Wayne's grandfather and father served in the military. His grandfather, Captain Anthony Wayne, a farmer by trade, commanded troops for King William III in the Battle of Boyne before leaving for the American Colonies. Captain Anthony Wayne and his family settled on an estate in Chester County in 1724, near what would become the town of Paoli. Their brick home, known as Waynesboro, is a designated historic site.

Wayne's father, Captain Isaac Wayne, remained in England for two years to finish his education. When he was 40 he married Elizabeth Iddlings of Philadelphia and his parents deeded their estate to him with the provision that he pay his parents an annuity for the remainder of their lives.

He built up the largest tannery in Pennsylvania and raised grain and feed crops. He was "a man of industry, admired by many and detested by some," according to information in the VanLeer papers in the Chester County Historical Society. He was commissioned in the militia and called out when Indian threats occurred. He served during the French and Indian War between 1755 and 1758.

Isaac and his wife had four children: daughters Hannah, Ann, and Margaret. Their only son, Anthony, was trained to be a surveyor at his uncle's private Philadelphia academy and later studied at the Academy and College of Philadelphia. He was a member of the class of 1765 but he did not earn a degree.

Appendix II
Tidbits

Names, Places, Events Connected with Wayne

- **Academy and College of Philadelphia** — Established by Benjamin Franklin and considered by many to be the first American University, now the University of Pennsylvania.
- **Beaver Wars** — Also called the Iroquois Wars or the French and Iroquois Wars. A series of conflicts from the mid 1640s to the mid 1680s. The Iroquois sought to expand their territory and monopolize the fur trade and the trade between European markets and the tribes of the western Great Lakes region. The conflict pitted the nations of the Iroquois Confederation, led by the dominant Mohawk, against the French-backed and largely Algonquian-speaking tribes of the Great Lakes region.
- **Blue Jacket** — Also known as Weyapiersenwah was a Shawnee war chief, well-known for his militant defense of Shawnee lands in Ohio Country. More than seven decades after he died in 1801, a story was published that claimed Blue Jacket was a white man, Marmaduke Van Swearingen, who had been captured and adopted by Shawnees in the 1770s. The story has since been debunked by known historical facts about the two men and DNA testing of their descendants.
- **Captain William Wells** — Injured at Battle of Fallen Timbers. Interpreter in Treaty of Greenville negotiations. Later served as Indian agent to the Miamis and requested a trading establishment of a trading post at Fort Wayne. Named Justice of the Peace by Territorial Governor William Henry Harrison. Sided with his father-in-law in Treaty of Vincennes but retained his position of Indian Agent.
- **Fort Green Ville** — Fort Greene Ville (now Greenville, Ohio), a pioneer fort built under General Anthony Wayne's command. At more than 55 acres this was the largest wooden fortification ever built. It was here that the Treaty of Greenville was

signed on August 3, 1795, bringing peace to the area and opening up the Northwest Territory for settlement. Fort Greene Ville was named for Wayne's friend General Nathanael Greene.

- **Fort Hamilton** — First in a chain of forts General St. Clair built north from Cincinnati in Indian country. Completed in October 1791. Served as a supply depot and garrison for American troops during the battle over the control of Western Ohio.

- **Fort Jefferson** — Build in 1791 by General Arthur St. Clair about five miles south of present-day Greenville, Ohio, and 45 miles north of Fort Hamilton. Within a month it became his refuge from a massive Indian army. Abandoned in 1796.

- **George Rogers Clark** — His celebrated captures of Kaskaskia (1778) and Vincennes (1779), greatly weakened British influence in the Northwest Territory. Because the British ceded the entire Northwest Territory to the United States in the 1783 Treaty of Paris, Clark has often been hailed as the "Conqueror of the Old Northwest."

- **Jay Treaty** — A treaty between the United States and Great Britain which averted war, solved many issues left over from the American Revolution, and opened ten years of largely peaceful trade in the midst of the French Revolutionary Wars.

- **Legion of the United States** — Secretary of War Henry Knox recommended recruiting and training a "Legion" that would combine all land combat arms of the day (cavalry, heavy and light infantry, artillery) into one efficient brigade-sized force that could be divided into stand-alone combined arms teams. Wayne was chosen to lead the new unit. Congress agreed to augment the small standing army until "the United States shall be at peace with the Indian tribes."

- **Logstown** — One of the large Indian towns on the upper Ohio in 1727-58. Important conferences were held here between the British, French, and Indians in the struggle for the Ohio country.

- **Ohio Indian Wars** — A series of struggles between white settlers from the United States and Indian residents of the Ohio Country in the years after the American Revolution.

- **Ohio Territory or Ohio Country** — Eighteenth century name for the area west of the Appalachian Mountains and in the region of the upper Ohio River south of Lake Erie. One of the first frontier regions and encompassed roughly the present-day states of Ohio, eastern Indiana, western Pennsylvania, and northwestern West Virginia. The issue of settlement in the region is considered by historians to have been a primary cause of the French and Indian War and a contributing factor to the American Revolutionary War.

- **Quebec Act** — Passed by the British Parliament to institute a permanent administration in Canada, gave the French Canadians complete religious freedom and restored the French form of civil law. It extended the Quebec boundaries to the Ohio River on the south and to the Mississippi River on the west.

- **Western Indian Confederacy** — Loose organization of North Americans in the Great Lakes region. Included tribes from the Shawnee, Council of the Three Fires (Ojibwe, Odawa, Potawatomi), Delaware, Miami, Kickapoo, Kaskaskia, Wabash Confederacy (Weas, Piankashaws and others), Chickamauga-Cherokee.

Appendix III
Test Your Knowledge

Questions

1. Did Colonel Anthony Wayne get involved in Indian affairs during the American Revolution?
   a. True
   b. False

2. Did General Anthony Wayne injure his leg on the eve of the Battle of Fallen Timbers?
   a. True
   b. False

3. When was General Anthony Wayne referred to as "Mad" by the local populace during?
   a. Battle of Fallen Timbers
   b. American Revolution

4. What was responsible for the Battle of Fallen Timbers?
   a. Tribal indifference among the local tribes
   b. Squatters settling into the lands that were unprotected.
   c. Settlers moving into the Northwest Territory.

5. In what Pennsylvania city is Wayne buried?
   a. Erie
   b. Radnor
   c. Philadelphia
   d. Waynesboro

6. Was General Wayne involved in the battles with the Indians in the Ohio Valley during the American Revolution?
   a. True
   b. False

7. What caused General Wayne's death?
   a. Battle injuries
   b. Gout
   c. Old Age

8. When did Little Turtle Die?
   a. 1809
   b. 1814
   c. 1812

9. When was the Treaty of Greenville signed?
   a. 1798
   b. 1796
   c. 1795

10. Why was Wayne chosen to lead the Legion of the United States?
    a. Experience
    b. Favoritism by President Washington

Answers:

1.
2. A
3. B
4. C
5. A and B
6. A
7. B
8. C
9. C
10. A
11. A.

Appendix IV
Glaciers Sculpt Landscape

Geological and Early Indian History of Ohio Territory reprinted from 'Expansion into the Connecticut Reserve' by Arthur Bauman)

Europeans were not the first to explore Ohio and its valuable waterways. Paleo-Indians began to enter the area approximately 11,000 years ago, just as the Laurentide ice sheet began its protracted retreat.

The ice sheet was the last major advance of continental glaciers in North America that created almost two-thirds of Ohio's present landscape. It had pushed into Ohio about 20,000 years ago, picking up rocks, pebbles, and other debris as it advanced south and west.

For the next 10,000 years, the glacier advanced and retreated, flattening and gouging the land. When the glacier that ranged from 1000 feet to one mile thick began to retreat and melt at the edges, the Great Lakes — as they are known today — began to take shape, starting in the Erie basin. Glacial deposits (till) remained to become the boulder clay deposit that makes up much of the original material for the soil for many miles south of present-day Lake Erie.

An ancient basin was exposed as the ice sheet retreated north, however glacial ice still blocked the St. Lawrence Seaway. Glacial melt water filled the lowland and formed lakes in front of the ice pack, including Glacial Lake Maumee, one of a few lakes/stages preceding modern-day Lake Erie.

For the next few thousand years, the lake levels in the Erie Basin fluctuated as the Wisconsin glacier slowly danced back and forth in its final phases. As the pressure from the great weight of the glacier eased, the land surface began to rise and the topography of the land gradually became what it is today.

Several sandy ridges formed along the shoreline of these lake stages, ridges which offered dry routes to Indians and early explorers. Some of these early trails would mark the way for primitive roads and the paved highways such as U.S. Route 20 west of Norwalk and east of Cleveland, Ohio.

Indians Here Before Europeans

Indians roamed and hunted the American continents, including parts of Ohio thousands of **years** before Europeans set sail on quests to find new routes, new lands, and riches. Archeological studies point to the possibility that people who lived in what is now Siberia crossed the Bering Strait to Alaska via an exposed land bridge. As they continued their slow trek, some headed south to the tip of South America, others scattered to other parts of the continents and islands.

In Ohio, the first inhabitants survived by hunting large game animals including wooly mammoths and mastodons. A group known as the Archaic people that hunted and gathered on the land disappeared around 1000 B.C. Between this time and 800 B.C., the Adena, cultivators and traders, inhabited the southern river valleys and introduced agriculture to the area; however, their lasting mark was the burial mounds that can still be found in those areas. The Hopewell — hunters, gathers, traders, and cultivators — moved into the area in about 100 B.C.

Sometime after A.D. 1000, the Whittlesey Focus People lived in villages that overlooked the river valleys of northern Ohio. The downfall of this group, as well as the little-known Erie tribe that lived on the southern shores of Lake Erie, coincided with the exploration by Europeans, who brought disease with them and supplied weapons to tribes such as the Iroquois.

Appendix V

Europeans Reach America
(Abridged version reprinted from 'Expansion into the Connecticut Reserve' by Arthur Bauman)

Driven by a combination of greed, curiosity, quest for knowledge, sense of adventure, and a desire to spread Christianity beyond European lands, explorers sailed southward and westward across the Atlantic Ocean in the fifteenth and sixteenth centuries.

Arabic traders' introduction of goods from other parts of the world broadened Europeans' outlook. Goods came from the Middle East, China, and India via Arabic intermediaries. Europeans yearned to cut out the middleman especially in the spice trade. Because spices helped to preserve meats, they were as valuable as gold or silver. In 1453 the land route from Europe to Asia was cut off by the Turkish Empire, which drove prices up. In hopes of finding a route to China and India as well as other riches the Portuguese headed south along Africa's west coast.

In 1488 Bartolomeu Dias sailed around the southern tip of Africa — the Cape of Good Hope, however after finding the passage to India he headed home. Ten years later, Vasco Da Gama became the first European to arrive in India via the Cape of Good Hope. Soon Portugal dominated the African trade routes and created a monopoly on the eastern spice trade.

Spanish explorers headed west across the Atlantic in an effort to get around the monopoly, to find gold and silver to pay for wars with the Turkish Empire, and to spread Christianity.

An eastern route to India was considered dangerous and ill-fated, not because of an outdated belief that explorers would fall off the edge of the earth, but because the ocean was too vast to cross and the chance of dehydration and/or starvation too great.

However, Genoese explorer Christopher Columbus was certain the earth was smaller than perceived and — almost a decade after being turned down by Portugal's king — persuaded King Ferdinand and Queen Isabella of Spain to fund a westward expedition.

Columbus landed in the Bahamas in October of 1492 and encountered native peoples.

While he mistakenly believed he'd found the East Indies — a belief he took to his grave — others believed he'd discovered a new continent, and coined it the "New World."

Controversy still surrounds Columbus' expeditions: Can someone discover a new land when it's already inhabited? Shouldn't Vikings get credit for their brief settlement of the northern land five hundred years earlier? The important thing is that Columbus's expedition brought attention to these lands and led to the European expansion and settlement of the Americas.

World's Unclaimed Lands Split

On June 7, 1494, the Portuguese and Spanish signed The Treaty of Tordesillas, dividing the world's unclaimed territories in half; Spain gained much more land than Portugal.

The ill-defined dividing line ran through the Atlantic Ocean and through a portion of South America. Spain gained the lands to the west, including all of North America and South America, with the exception Brazil. In addition to the small chunk of South America, Portugal gained Africa and India.

The treaty created an effective blockade of these new markets — a blockade that the two Catholic countries maintained for much of the sixteenth century.

Portugal focused on navigation. Spain sent waves of explorers into South America in search of gold, slaves, lucrative trade routes, and fame; it became the predominant European power in the southern continent. Hernando Cortes landed in Veracruz and conquered the Aztecs of Mexico in the 1520s. By 1532 Francisco Pizarro had conquered the Incas in Peru.

Early on Spain had a dominant presence in North America. After some initial struggles, Spain claimed Florida and later settled the Southwest as a part of its vast empire.

Spanish explorers made a few attempts to venture into the South Central and Southeast portions of the United States, but they only served to antagonize the Indians and settlers opted to not move into these areas.

The French Arrive

In hopes of finding a Northwest Passage to Asia, France ignored the treaty and began to explore the northern areas that had been neglected by their longtime Spanish enemies.

In 1524 or 1525, Italian explorer Giovanni da Verrazano journeyed to the New World, landing on the North Carolina Coast. When he reached the Outer Banks of North Carolina, he mistook present-day Pamlico Sound for the Pacific Ocean. Based on his observations, mapmakers drew North America as a long, narrow isthmus, with its two parts connected by a narrow piece of land. That belief remained intact for more than a century.

As Verrazano continued north along the coast, he landed on the shores of the New York and Narragansett bays, becoming the first recorded European to visit this area. His report to King Francis I provided the first description of the Northeastern Coast.

Between 1534 and 1542 Jacques Cartier explored the present-day Gulf of St. Lawrence and the St. Lawrence River, called it New France and claimed much of present-day Canada for France. With the help of Indian guides on his second trip, he followed the river until he reached a hill, which Cartier named Mont Real. From the summit, Cartier spotted impassable rapids on the river, as well as land — instead of a passageway — stretching out as far as he could see.

Although he had not found a western route to Asia, he had discovered a valuable waterway.

His expeditions kick-started possible European settlement in the region. An initial try at establishing a colony at Cape Rouge failed in the 1540s. However, fur traders established outposts along the St. Lawrence waterways, securing the lands for France.

The Jesuit order, founded in the mid-1500s followed the French explorers and set up parishes among the Indians. The fur traders and Jesuits recognized the importance of maintaining good relationships with the Indians to ensure survival in this wild land.

Between 1603 and 1635, Samuel de Champlain made several voyages to North America and accomplished such feats as:
- Mapping the Atlantic Coast from Cape Cod to the Bay of Fundy off the northern coast of what is now Maine and extending into Canada.
- Finding Indian tribes that would trade furs for French goods.
- Establishing outposts, most notably Quebec City in 1608.

In 1611, he managed to negotiate the rapids and became the first European (apart from Étienne Brûlé, whom Champlain had sent into the wilderness to live among the tribes) to navigate the portion of the St. Lawrence River and tributaries that led to the continent's interior.

The French explorers recognized the importance of forming alliances with the native peoples, so Champlain forged bonds with the Algonquin and Huron tribes against the Iroquois Confederacy. After battles with the Iroquois on the eastern end of Lake Ontario and near the lake that now bears his name, Champlain gained control of the St. Lawrence region. Hoping to make the Quebec settlement his own personal trading post and rake in the profits, Champlain discouraged any kind of large-scale colonization of New France.

When King Louis XIV's rule began in 1661, he viewed New France as more than a giant trading post — he wanted to encourage settlement in order to create an international empire.

LaSalle Settles in Quebec; Dutch Arrive

René Robert Cavelier, Sieur de La Salle He set sail for New France in 1660 and was granted land near the La Chine Rapids above Montreal. By 1669, La Salle had heard about a great river system that could be the elusive passage to the South Sea (and Asia) and set out to find it.

La Salle crossed Lake Ontario, Lake Erie, and possibly made his way fifteen to twenty-one miles from the Great Lakes to the Ohio River, at present-day Louisville, Kentucky when his followers abandoned him and turned back before reaching his goal.

The discovery of the "father of all rivers" (the Mississippi) was left to Louis Joliet and Jesuit priest Jacques Marquette in 1673. La Salle, with permission of the king, continued to explore the waterways. He envisioned trading outposts along the Mississippi River. By 1682 La Salle made his way to the Mississippi River and reached the Gulf of Mexico near Biloxi, Mississippi.

He claimed the lands surrounding the river and all its tributaries — in essence all the territory between the Appalachian and the Rocky Mountains — for France.

The Netherlands joined the illusive search for the passage to Asia in the seventeenth century. In 1609 Englishman Henry Hudson, in the service of the Dutch East India Company, sailed to America and up the river that now bears his name and claimed everything from the surrounding river valley to present-day Albany, New York.

He had not found a shortcut to Asia, but he did provide the Netherlands with a claim to rich fur-bearing lands. The Dutch West India Trading Company (founded in 1621) established New Netherlands in 1623 and built a trading post at Fort Orange (Albany). In 1624, they purchased Manhattan Island from the Manhattan Indians for goods in the equivalent of approximately $24 and founded New Amsterdam (New York). The Dutch also briefly controlled areas including the present-day states of Delaware, Connecticut, and New Jersey.

English Interest in America Grows

For the first half of sixteenth century, England had no real presence in the Americas even though they stepped foot here before the French. After hearing about Columbus' discoveries, King Henry VII sent John Cabot across the Atlantic in 1497 in the search of the Northwest Passage to Asia.

Cabot landed in Canada, possibly Newfoundland or Cape Breton. On his second voyage in 1498, he and four of his five ships disappeared en route (the fifth ship had turned back for repairs). England's exploration stopped until the final decades of the sixteenth century.

Queen Elizabeth I pushed English and Dutch explorers, including Sir John Hawkins and Sir Francis Drake, to take to the sea and become privateers (pirates). Drake sailed around the tip of South America to the shores of California, claiming western lands for England. On that trip he continued his westward progress and became the first Englishman to sail around the world.

Hoping to find the key to the trading empire in North America, the queen granted a charter to Sir Humphrey Gilbert to settle lands not claimed by Christians. Gilbert reached the shores of St. John's Bay, Newfoundland, in 1583, however on his return trip, his overloaded ship sunk. The charter passed to Sir Walter Raleigh (Gilbert's half-brother), who never sailed to America.

In 1584, two ships sailed to the Outer Banks of North Carolina to scout locations for future colonies. Upon returning, they provided enthusiastic and positive reports about the indigenous peoples and the land, which Raleigh named Virginia, after the "Virgin Queen," Elizabeth.

A small group of settlers headed for Virginia in 1585 and established a colony at Roanoke. Sir Francis Drake stopped at the colony about a year later, found the colonists starving, and returned them to England.

Raleigh planned another settlement; this time he instructed the captains to settle at Chesapeake Bay. One of the captains disregarded the advice and 117 men, women, and children settled on Roanoke Island. After a couple of weeks, John White, the colony's leader, returned to England to get supplies after supply ships had been delayed because of attacks by the Spanish Armada. White's attempt to return to the colony was delayed until 1590, but by then the colonists had disappeared.

England Realizes Need to Expand

England needed to succeed in its expansion across the Atlantic. The medieval feudal system had been replaced with a peasant class that England had trouble feeding. In addition, the Renaissance had created a merchant/artesian class that yearned for new markets.

In 1606 King James I granted charters to establish colonies to two merchant groups — the Virginia Company of London in southern Virginia and the Plymouth Company of London in northern Virginia, which then encompassed what today is 13 New England states.

By May 1607, the Virginia Company had entered the Chesapeake Bay, sailed along a river, and established England's first permanent colony, Jamestown, on a tract of swampland.

The 105 settlers who reached the shores were a mix of rich and poor, the latter of whom agreed to become indentured servants for seven years in exchange for passage to America.

Almost immediately the colony was in trouble. It was too late to plant crops; the rich settlers didn't know how or want to work; malaria and dysentery spread through the area.

The local tribe was unfriendly toward and suspicious of these newcomers and attacked the settlement during the first few weeks. Within six months, about half the settlers were dead from disease or starvation.

Smith Keeps Colony Alive

John Smith, initially hired in order to supervise the military defense, kept the colony alive. He became friends with Powhatan, the local Indian chief and obtained enough food to feed the remaining colonists. In September 1608, Smith was elected president f the local council and enforced a rigid discipline, declaring, "He who will not work, neither shall he eat." The colony had to find a way to make a profit. So far they had found nothing marketable in the New World.

In 1613 and 1614, John Rolfe produced a variety of tobacco that became popular in Europe. Its popularity enticed more settlers to venture to the New World to get rich.

The Plymouth Company established a colony (Popham) in Maine the same year as the Jamestown settlement, however, over the course of the next year all the colonists abandoned it and returned to England. In 1609 King James gave the Virginia Company exclusive rights to the previously shared territory, as well as the rights of the land within the parallels from "sea to sea."

Settlers Seek Religious Freedom

It would be 1620 before the Plymouth Company would reorganize under the name Plymouth Council for New England. King James granted a charter which gave the council the lands from the 40th parallel to the 48th parallel (including current-day Nova Scotia and New Brunswick) and from "sea to sea."

The settlement was funded by the Virginia Company. Those in Virginia Company's earlier colony (Jamestown) came to the new world mostly in search of trade and riches; those who came to settle Plymouth Colony were looking for a place where they could practice their faith.

The Church of England broke from the Catholic Church in 1533 and made constitutional changes — including one which declared the Church of England was a part of the state, and thereby governed by the monarch, however it remained more Catholic than Protestant — even reuniting with the Catholic church for a brief time in the 1550s.

Change Spurs Separation

The seeds of religious separation had been planted and would eventually spur British residents to seek out new land where they could worship in the way they wished.

The Separatists (later also called Pilgrims), shunned all the ritual and symbols used in the Anglican Church and wished to worship in a simple manner. They believed it would be easier to separate from the state church, rather than implement all the reforms needed.

The Separatists, a group of mostly impoverished farmers and craftsmen, moved first to Holland in 1608 to avoid persecution. While able to grow up with a little more religious freedom there, concern arose about the children being influenced more by Dutch culture than British.

In 1617, the Separatists decided to find a home where they could worship as they saw fit, but keep their English identity; they looked to America. In 1620 the Separatists received patents to colonize the Virginia Company's northern region — the Hudson River area — and boarded the *Speedwell* for a journey to England, where the ship would meet up with the *Mayflower*.

Both ships were supposed to sail to America, however the *Speedwell* was declared unseaworthy. Joining the Separatists were the Strangers — non-Separatists who wanted to travel to America; they were needed to meet the required number of passengers necessary for the trip.

Mayflower Sails from England

The *Mayflower* departed from Plymouth, England, on September 16, 1620, with 102 passengers, only 41 of them Separatists. All would be classified as Pilgrims in later years.

After 65 days, the Pilgrims landed near Cape Cod, well north of the Virginia Company's control. It's uncertain whether the landing was due to rough seas off Nantucket or an attempt for more independence. When it came time to land some who had promised to be indentured servants decided they were not under English law and did not have to honor their promises.

The rebellion led the leaders to draw up the "Mayflower Compact," which stated the Pilgrims would create their own laws and elect their own leaders. It was the first document in America that ensured the establishment of government included the concept "for the people, by the people."

The settlement struggled to survive and had only 300 settlers by 1630, but it encouraged the settlement of other areas, including the Massachusetts bays by the Puritans.

Puritans, like the Separatists, saw the state church as corrupt. However the Puritans believed they did not have to break from the Anglican Church — they just needed to purify it. Some followers thought the only way to reform the Church of England was to leave England. They hoped they'd form colonies that would prove to be a shining example of the true way to God.

By 1630 a group of Puritans, having secured a charter from the Massachusetts Land Company, established settlements in Boston and Salem. The Massachusetts Colony, unlike Plymouth's, had more colonists and was backed by those with wealth.

Colonies Begin Expansion

As the original settlements thrived, more people headed across the Atlantic to the new shores. New colonies emerged — some, like Connecticut and New Hampshire, as expansions of Puritan settlements.

The Puritans were intolerant of others who wished to worship in other ways. This led other migrants to seek out other lands where they could worship as they saw fit.

In his travels in the Massachusetts Colony, Reverend Roger Williams, advocated unpopular — even considered heretical by some — opinions including notions that England could not just take lands from the Indians without a treaty and that the church and state should be separate.

Leaders of the Puritan government tried to send Williams back to England, but found safety among some of the Indians he'd befriended, purchased land from them, and founded Providence, which became the first settlement in Rhode Island — a place that welcomed any protestant sect.

In 1632 George Calvert, a convert to Roman Catholicism, obtained a charter from King Charles I to establish a colony (Maryland) north of Virginia. The charter did not prohibit the formation of non-Protestant churches in the area. Roman Catholics, who were being persecuted in England, were encouraged to migrate to the settlement along with Protestants.

Soon, however, Protestants outnumbered the Catholics in the region, and the Catholics were facing the same oppression as they had in England.

War Slows Expansion

During the 1640s, the American colonization slowed due to England's civil war between King Charles I (and later his son) and Parliament. When the war was over, the monarchy had been overthrown, King Charles I had been beheaded, and his son, Charles II, had fled to France. Oliver Cromwell had been named Lord Protector and ruled England, Scotland, and Ireland. Shortly after Cromwell's death in 1660, Charles II reclaimed the throne.

Wanting to expand England's empire in America, Charles II granted the land south of Virginia and north of Spanish Florida to eight of his wealthy supporters. Named Carolina, the area was almost always governed in two parts and officially separated into North Carolina and South Carolina in the early 1700s.

King Charles II set his sights on the Dutch-controlled territory between New England and Virginia and by 1664 the Dutch lands had fallen under English control. Charles gave the region between Maryland and New England to his brother, the Duke of York (later King James II) and New Amsterdam was renamed New York. James gave the land that would later become New Jersey to a couple of men who had been steadfast supporters during the English Civil War.

The Religious Society of Friends, more commonly known as the Quakers, began practicing their peace-oriented faith in mid-seventeenth Century England, where its followers were soon persecuted for refusing to take an oath to anyone. Quakerism had been banned in some of colonial settlements; some were executed for their beliefs.

In 1681 William Penn received a grant from King Charles II for the area west of New Jersey, which included present-day Pennsylvania. A year later present-day Delaware was incorporated into the charter to provide access to the sea; it became a separate colony in 1701. The region became a place where Quakers could freely practice their faith. The opportunity to worship freely enticed other groups such as Huguenots (French Protestants) and Lutherans to migrate to the area.

In 1732 a proprietary colony was set up by the King George II under James Oglethorpe for those imprisoned for debt. Oglethorpe envisioned the colony as a place that rehabilitated prisoners could embark in a fresh start. Laws in Georgia Colony outlawed rum and slavery and put a limit on the amount of land an individual could have.

It's doubtful that King George II had such altruistic ideas for Georgia. It's more likely that he saw it primarily as a buffer between the English colonies and Spanish-controlled Florida. Without support from England, Oglethorpe's dreams for the colony fell apart and soon it was no different than any other southern colony.

The colonization of America had begun. The next hundred years, marred by several wars stemming from territorial disputes and cries for freedom, would forever change the world.

Select Reference Material

Listed here are the publications and many of the general Websites consulted in writing this book. This is not a complete record of all resources; it simply reflects the substance and range of background reading on which this book is based

Story:
Anthony Wayne
http://www.infoplease.com/biography/us/congress/wayne-anthony.html
http://www.biographybase.com/biography/Wayne_Anthony.html
http://www.ushistory.org/valleyforge/served/wayne.html
http://en.wikipedia.org/wiki/Anthony_Wayne
http://www.nndb.com/people/074/000049924/
http://www.biographybase.com/biography/Wayne_Anthony.html
http://americanrevwar.homestead.com/files/wayne.htm
http://www.ushistory.org/valleyforge/served/wayne.html
http://www.ushistory.org/paoli/history/waynemad.htm
http://www.bing.com/reference/semhtml/Anthony_Wayne

Geology
Dyke, A.S.; Prest, V.K. (1987). "Late Wisconsinan and Holocene History of the Laurentide Ice Sheet". *Gèographie physique et Quaternaire* **41** (2): 237–263.
http://www.erudit.org/revue/GPQ/1987/v41/n2/032681ar.html.
Bauman, Arthur (XXXX) "Expansion into Connecticut Western Reserve"
http://en.wikipedia.org/wiki/Cypress_Hills_%28Canada%29
http://en.wikipedia.org/wiki/Laurentide_ice_sheet
http://www.ohiohistorycentral.org/subcategory.php?c=NH&s=GEOG

Military History
http://www.bing.com/reference/semhtml/Fort_Miami_%28Ohio%29?fwd=1&src=abop&qpvt=fort+miami&q=fort+miami
http://en.wikipedia.org/wiki/Fort_Prince_George
http://militaryhistory.about.com/od/americanrevolution/ig/Valley-Forge/Baron-von-Steuben.htm

http://en.wikipedia.org/wiki/Battle_of_Monmouth
http://militaryhistory.about.com/od/americanrevolution/ig/Valley-Forge/Baron-von-Steuben.htm
http://revolutionarywararchives.org/stonypoint.html
http://en.wikipedia.org/wiki/Battle_of_Stony_Point
http://www.revolutionaryday.com/usroute9w/stonypoint/default.htm
http://en.wikipedia.org/wiki/Treaty_of_Mississinwas
http://www.philaprintshop.com/frchintx.html
http://en.wikipedia.org/wiki/Little_Turtlehttp://en.wikipedia.org/wiki/Beaver_Wars
http://www.encyclopedia.com/topic/1774_Quebec_Act.aspx
http://www.bing.com/reference/semhtml/William_Wells_%28soldier%29?fwd=1&qpvt=captain+william+wells&src=abop&q=captain+william+wellshttp://sinclair.quarterman.org/history/mod/battleofwabash.html
http://en.wikipedia.org/wiki/Battle_of_the_Wabash
http://americanrevwar.homestead.com/files/GREENE.HTM
http://en.wikipedia.org/wiki/Charles_Lee_%28general%29
http://mysite.verizon.net/vze4xzhn/trents_history.htm
http://www.bing.com/reference/search?q=Jay+Treaty&go=&form=FDNF
http://lanepl.org/blount/jbplaces/documents/A5EBD2139DD7DE021EA706FD4A667042BF42FCBB.html
http://en.wikipedia.org/wiki/Fort_Ticonderoga
http://militaryhistory.about.com/b/2007/06/08/american-revolution-battle-of-trois-rivieres.htm
http://www.ushistory.org/march/phila/paoli_6.htm
http://www.ushistory.org/march/phila/germantown.htm
http://en.wikipedia.org/wiki/Battle_of_Germantown
http://www.sonofthesouth.net/revolutionary-war/battles/stony-point.htm
http://www.philaprintshop.com/frchintx.html
http://en.wikipedia.org/wiki/Treaty_of_Fort_McIntosh

Ohio Territory History
Ohio History Central. "Wisconsin Glacier." July 13, 2007, VanLeer Papers, Chester County Historical Society
http://www.ohiohistorycentral.org/entry.php?rec=2893
http://www.ohiohistorycentral.org/entry.php?rec=1424
http://www.answers.com/topic/arthur-st-clair
http://sinclair2.quarterman.org/history/mod/battleofwabash.html
http://www.shelbycountyhistory.org/schs/indians/coljohnhardin.htm
http://en.wikipedia.org/wiki/Battle_of_the_Wabash
http://www.electricscotland.com/history/world/bios/stclair_general.htm
http://www.ohiohistorycentral.org/entry.php?rec=703
http://visitdefianceohio.com/?page_id=56
http://www.ohiohistorycentral.org/entry.php?rec=527
http://www.ushistory.org/paoli/history/wayneburied.htm
http://www.historicforks.org/miami/

http://www.historicforks.org/buildlings/buildings.html#ChiefsHouse
http://www.ohiohistorycentral.org/entry.php?rec=606&nm=Miami-Indians
http://en.wikipedia.org/wiki/Ohio_Country
http://www.ohiohistorycentral.org/entry.php?rec=527
http://www.ohiohistorycentral.org/entry.php?rec=197
http://en.wikipedia.org/wiki/Legionville
http://www.bing.com/reference/semhtml/Firelands?fwd=1&src=abop&qpvt=firelands&q=fi
relands
http://www.shelbycountyhistory.org/schs/indians/fortjefferson.htm
http://www.ohiohistorycentral.org/entry.php?rec=707
http://www.ohiohistorycentral.org/entry.php?rec=483
http://www.ohiohistorycentral.org/entry.php?rec=780&nm=Ohio-Country
http://www.u-s-history.com/pages/h1016.html

Index